JOINING

The United States Coast Guard

JOINING THE MILITARY

A McFarland Handbook Series
by Snow Wildsmith

Joining the United States Coast Guard

A Handbook

SNOW WILDSMITH

JOINING THE MILITARY, 3

McFarland & Company, Inc., Publishers
Jefferson, North Carolina, and London

LIBRARY OF CONGRESS CATALOGUING-IN-PUBLICATION DATA

Wildsmith, Snow, 1973–
Joining the United States Coast Guard : a handbook / Snow Wildsmith.
        p.   cm. — (Joining the military ; 3)
Includes bibliographical references and index.

ISBN 978-0-7864-4760-2
softcover : acid free paper ∞

1. United States. Coast Guard — Vocational guidance.   I. Title.
VG53.W55 2012   363.28'602373 — dc23   2012010081

BRITISH LIBRARY CATALOGUING DATA ARE AVAILABLE

On the cover: *inset* seal of the United States Coast Guard;
photograph crewmembers of the Coast Guard cutters *Boutwell* and
Sherman stand at attention during a presentation of colors for the
change of homeport ceremony aboard the *Sherman* at U.S. Naval Base
San Diego, July 29, 2011 (United States Coast Guard photograph
by Petty Officer 2nd Class Sondra-Kay Kneen-Rivera)

Manufactured in the United States of America

*McFarland & Company, Inc., Publishers
Box 611, Jefferson, North Carolina 28640
www.mcfarlandpub.com*

For my father,
HMCM Donald P. Wildsmith, USN (Ret.),
with love and respect for all he has given
for me and for his country.

Acknowledgments

This book could not have been written without the support of the United States Coast Guard. Thank you to all of the Guardians who took the time out of their busy days to answer my questions, supply me with needed information, tour me around recruit training, and generally help me out with whatever I needed.

Thank you also to librarian and friend Emily Leachman for proofreading my rough drafts and making suggestions for improvement. I owe a debt of gratitude to all of my friends and family who supported me during the writing process, especially to my ever-patient and ever-loving husband Barry.

Table of Contents

Read This First

Patriotism. Money for college. Family tradition. Job training. Adventure. Secure employment. Travel. Service to others. The opportunity to do something different. There are as many reasons to join the military as there are people in the military. Some people want to make a full career out of their military service. Some just want to get in, do their time, and get the benefits they've earned. Others are in the middle — they aren't sure where they want to go after the military or how long they want to spend in the service, but they think it might be a good job for the time being.

Whether you are certain that you want to enter the military or you are just curious and want more information, you still will need to consider a lot of factors before you join. This series of books is designed to help you look at all of your options to see whether or not military service is right for you and, if so, to help you figure out which branch of the service is for you. There is one book for each branch of the service: Air Force, Army, Coast Guard, Marine Corps, and Navy. Within each book, there are sections on:

- Looking at your personality to see if you will fit the military lifestyle
- Talking with a recruiter to find out what the service offers and what they expect from you in return
- How enlisting works and what you need to do during the process
- Taking the Armed Services Vocational Aptitude Battery test
- Preparing for recruit training (also called basic training) mentally, physically, emotionally, and socially

1

- What happens during basic training
- Books, DVDs, and websites with more information on joining the military, military history, and life in the military

Joining the military is a major lifestyle change, one which will affect not only you, but also your family and your friends. You'll need to think long and hard about all of your options and the choice you are about to make. These books will give you the basic information you need, but you should know that every individual's enlistment and training experience is different, shaped by their personality, education, goals, and interests. Additionally, the branches of the military are constantly evaluating and adjusting their policies and procedures to meet their current needs. The military personnel you speak with during your time considering military service will have up-to-date information about enlistment and training.

Whatever branch you choose to serve in, however long your term of enlistment, whichever occupational specialty you pick — you will be part of something larger than you. Deciding to become a serviceman or servicewoman can be the best thing that ever happened to you as it guides the rest of your life in ways you never expected.

ONE

Thinking About Joining the Military

Things to Consider for Potential Enlistees

There are many big decisions people make over their lifetime. "Should I go to college or get a job?" "Who will I marry?" "Will I have children?" "Where will I live?" Deciding to join the military is one of those momentous decisions. If you decide to join, you will be committing yourself to service to the government for at least eight years — the length of your active duty contract plus the years you are obligated to spend in the Individual Ready Reserve, where you aren't actively doing military training and work, but can still be called up by the government.

Because you will be making a legal, binding contract that cannot be gotten out of easily, you must consider all of the factors carefully before deciding to enlist in the military. Take your time, do your research, and, most of all, don't let anyone pressure you to join or not to join. This is your life and the decision should be yours.

Pros and Cons

The first thing to consider are the positives and negatives of joining the military — the pros and cons. What will you gain by joining and what will you have to sacrifice?

PROS

- Employment — joining the military will give you a job with a steady, guaranteed income as well as health insurance, housing, and a clothing allowance

- Training — the military offers training on a wide variety of jobs, and you will be paid, fed, clothed, and housed while you are training
- Education — in addition to the job training offered by the military, you will also earn money to help pay for future education; you can even start college and earn a degree while serving in the military — sometimes completely paid for by the military
- Travel — service in the military pretty much guarantees travel, both in the U.S. and around the world
- Purpose — military service is just that: service; you will be serving your country and working for something bigger than just you

CONS

- War — the first and most important job of the military is to protect the United States; by joining you face the very real possibility of ending up in a war zone
- Freedom — by joining the military you will be voluntarily giving up a good amount of your personal freedom for the regimen of military life
- Time — serving in the military means a lot of hard work, often including long hours and even days, weeks, or months away from friends and family
- Training and Education — there are a lot of training and education opportunities in the military, but the military's interest is to train you in what they need to you do, so your education desires come second if they don't fit with current military needs
- Travel — you will travel and you will have some say in where you travel to, but not always; if some get to serve in Paris or Hawaii, many serve in much less glamorous locales

These are some of the major factors to consider as you begin to think about possible military service. As you learn more about the military, you'll also need to consider whether or not you are a good candidate for the military and whether or not the military can help you achieve the goals you have set for your life.

6

Your Personality, Your Goals, and Your Future Aspirations

The military has its own goals and its own direction for the future and so should you. It is important that you think about what your goals are before deciding if military service is right for you. If you don't have goals planned out, now is the time to make them. Start thinking about what you might want to accomplish in the future. The military will be happy to use your hard work to accomplish its goals, but if its goals are not the same as what you want to do with your life, then your time of service will be one of frustration.

Additionally, you should think about the military lifestyle and whether or not it fits with your personality. The military is regimented, ordered, and focused on teamwork. If you are a rugged individualist, then military service might not be an easy job for you as your superiors will try to change that mindset.

This book and the others in this series focus on enlisted careers in the military. "Enlisted" means those servicemen and women who are not officers. Enlisted personnel are responsible for the daily operations of the military, whereas officers are the command personnel, the ones who give the orders. That doesn't mean that enlisted service members don't lead. There are a lot of opportunities for enlisted men and women to learn and practice leadership skills, starting as early as basic training. The higher ranks of enlisted personnel are called "non-commissioned officers" and they take on many of the leadership roles in the military. You do not need a college degree to enlist in the military, but you do need one to be commissioned — meaning appointed — as an officer. That is another factor to keep in mind as you are deciding if a military career is right for you.

MILITARY QUESTIONNAIRE

The following questionnaire will help you think about your lifestyle, your personality, and your future to see if they might fit well with the military.

Read each statement and see if "yes"—it does agree with you, "no"—it does not agree with you, or "maybe"—it sort of agrees with you or you aren't sure. There are no right or wrong answers. These are just factors to consider. The notes after each statement will help you see how that statement does or does not fit with a possible career in the military.

YES NO MAYBE I am interested in serving in the military because of patriotic reasons.

- This is a great reason to join the military. Having a high degree of patriotism means that you'd be willing to offer up your life to protect and serve your country. But there are other ways that patriotic people can serve the United States, so if you aren't certain that military service is for you, consider non-military service options.

YES NO MAYBE I am interested in serving in the military because I want to give back to others.

- Also a good reason to join the military, but again, if you are positive that you wish to serve others, but uncertain about the military, there are other options that will allow you to help out.

YES NO MAYBE I am interested in serving in the military because my father/mother/other family member served.

- This is another good reason for joining. If you were raised in a military family or if you grew up hearing stories about a family member's military service, then you will probably be proud to serve and carry on a family tradition. Make sure, though, that you get the most recent information on military life and make sure that your personality and goals are as compatible with military service as your family member's were. Also be sure that you are not joining because....

YES NO MAYBE My father/mother/other family member says that I have to join the military.

- DO NOT allow yourself to be forced or coerced into military

Serving in the Coast Guard is an excellent way to support the people of the United States (Official U.S. Coast Guard photograph by Petty Officer 2nd Class Patrick Kelley).

service. It is your life and your decision. No one else can make it for you.

YES   NO   MAYBE   I want to serve in the military, but only part-time, and/or I don't want to have to move away from where I am living.

- Then you will want to consider enlisting as a reservist. Service men and women in the reserves serve one weekend a month and two weeks out of the year, during which time they train with a local unit. Reservists are still members of the military and are subject to the same regulations and laws as active-duty service members, as well as receiving many of the same benefits that active-duty personnel receive. You should know, however, that as a reservist you can be called up to active duty for a period of time ranging from several weeks to several years in order to fight in war. And job choices in the reserves can be limited, as they are almost always assigned based on the needs of the reserve unit with which you will serve.

YES   NO   MAYBE   I want to serve in the military, but only for my initial term of enlistment (usually four years).

- It is possible to sign up for a four year stint in the military, complete your time, and then choose not to reenlist. However, there are some factors to keep in mind. First of all, even after you finish your term and leave the military, you are still part of the military until you have completed a full eight years of service. The enlistment contract that you sign when you join the military makes it clear that you are obligated for those eight years and that any time you don't spend as active duty must be spent in the inactive reserves, called the Individual Ready Reserve (IRR). While you are in the IRR, you can still be called up to duty if the military needs you.
- If the military still needs your services at the end of your enlistment term, it can prevent you from leaving. A program called "Stop Loss" allows the military, during times of conflict, to prevent you for up to one year from leaving at your normal separation date. The military has been using this program during the conflicts in Iraq and Afghanistan to ensure that personnel who are doing specific jobs are still around to do those jobs when the military needs them.

YES   NO   MAYBE   I have dropped out of or not finished high school or I have my GED or I am considering dropping out of high school.

- Today's military wants service members who have at least finished high school. If you are still in school, you will need to finish and graduate, trying for the best grades you can get. If you have dropped out, you will have to get a GED in order to be eligible to enlist. However, every branch of the military has strict limitations on how many people they will accept with

GEDs each year and those candidates must score higher grades on the Armed Services Vocational Aptitude Battery (ASVAB) test which all potential enlistees must take. (More on the ASVAB in Part Three.) Your best bet is to get your GED and also have at least 15 hours of college credit. With most branches of the military, that will put you on the same footing as a high school graduate.

YES   NO   MAYBE   I am interested in serving in the military because I have nothing better to do with my life.
- On the one hand, this is a terrible reason for joining the military. You need to think a lot more about what you are capable of and where you see yourself in the future. Joining the military should not be a spur of the moment decision or one made because you are bored or directionless. You must carefully consider all aspects of an enlistment decision and look for all options available to you, even if you aren't sure right now what those options are. Careful research will help you make the right choice for your future.
- On the other hand, the military is willing to take your raw material and mold you into the warrior it needs. If you are open to allowing yourself to be guided, the military can help you find a job and training while you figure out who you are and what you want out of life. Just be sure that you are willing to give them eight years of your life to do it.

YES   NO   MAYBE   I am interested in serving in the military for the education benefits: money for college.
- Money is available for those who have served in the military and who now want to attend college. Make sure that you get information on how long you'll need to serve, what types of service are eligible, how much money you'll receive, and how and when that money can be used in the future. The next chapter offers information on the benefits of enlisting, including education benefits, and military recruiters will always be able to

give you the most up-to-date information available. (More on talking to recruiters in Part Three.)

YES   NO   MAYBE   I am interested in serving in the military for the job benefits: training, housing, etc.
- The military is a great way to learn a career and get paid while you're learning. Remember, though, that the military's selection of jobs in the fields which interest you may be limited and/or the military may or may not find you qualified for training in the job you want. If you can't get the training that you're interested in, you can see if the military offers another job which you would be interested in doing or you will have to look for civilian training in the career you want.

YES   NO   MAYBE   I have computer, mechanical, scientific, medical, administrative, or technical interests or skills that I want to make into a career and need to be trained in.
- These are great skills to hone in the military, though if you aren't planning on making the military a life-long career, then you will want to look for a military job which will allow you to learn skills that you can use in civilian life after your term of service is up. Check out one of the books or websites on military jobs in the appendix under "For More Information — Career Planning." They will help give you an idea of what military jobs are available and how they correspond to civilian work.

YES   NO   MAYBE   I have artistic interests or skills that I want to make into a career and need training in.
- Many people assume that the military only offers technical jobs, but if you want a more artistic career, the military has jobs for you as well. There are some spots for chefs, musicians, graphic designers, and more in the military, but the number of these jobs available can be lower than other positions, so competition is often higher.

- If you are willing to delay your artistic career in favor of serving in the military, you can choose a different career path during your service and then use your educational benefits to study your art once you have left or retired from the military.

YES   NO   MAYBE   I want a job that can become a lifetime career.
- The military is a good possibility for a lifetime career. As long as you are willing to apply yourself to your work, you can retire after 20 or 30 years and still be young enough to enjoy yourself and even start a second career while also collecting your military retirement pay.

YES   NO   MAYBE   I need a job for now, but I am not sure that I want to make a life-long commitment.
- The military is also a great choice for those who want a job for now, but who aren't sure that they want to stay in that career forever. You'll have the opportunity to reenlist every few years and can decide at that time if you want to stay in or get out. If you decide to stay in, though, you're bound for the next few years, so the military is not a good choice for those who like to switch jobs every year. Consider what job you want to do and think about if you'll want to do it in the military for at least two, four, or six years, depending on how long your term of enlistment is.

YES   NO   MAYBE   I want a 9-to-5 job with a set schedule.
- Then the military is probably not for you. Military jobs can be orderly and set, with regular hours, but many of them involve working varied hours and an ever-shifting schedule.

YES   NO   MAYBE   I am a hard worker.
- If you are willing to work hard, then military life may be a good fit for you. Your superiors will want to see you giving your all and the service personnel you work with want to be working with someone who can be there for them to help carry the load.

YES   NO   MAYBE   I want to push myself and see what I can accomplish.

- A stint of service in the military is a good personal challenge. During your initial recruit training, what your instructors will want is for you to give your best effort, especially when you think you can't. Later on in military service, your superiors and your fellow service personnel will want you to be eager to try new things, to learn, and to grow in your chosen field.

YES   NO   MAYBE   I like physical exercise and activity.

- The military requires that its service members be physically fit in order for them to perform their jobs to the best of their ability. Each branch of the service has its own requirements for physical fitness standards, so you will need to consider whether or not you are able to meet or able to train to meet those standards.

YES   NO   MAYBE   I like being outdoors and/or don't mind roughing it.

- While not all military jobs are outdoors, at least during recruit training you will be hiking, camping, learning to navigate outdoor terrain, participating in warfare simulations, etc. If you are sent to war — which is a possibility for everyone who enlists in the military — then you will be faced with living in a variety of terrains, in tents and in other rough conditions. Even those personnel who live on ships or in barracks often live in close quarters with others and don't have many of the luxuries civilians may be used to.

YES   NO   MAYBE   I always do things my way and don't like taking orders from anyone.

- A big part of military life is taking orders, even if those orders seem to make no sense or go against what you may want to do. While the military does train its service members to think ethically and morally and to make judgments for themselves, it also expects people to follow orders and to work with others.

YES   NO   MAYBE   I want to be a leader or a manager.
- Military service is an excellent way to gain leadership experience. The military trains all its service personnel to take on leadership roles, even as early as boot camp. You have to be willing to start at the bottom, though. Don't assume that you will lead right away. You have to learn how and you have to earn the right to lead.

YES   NO   MAYBE   I work and play well with others.
- Teamwork is a major part of military life. Not only will you be working closely with others in your unit, you will also be living in close quarters — sometimes very close. The military needs people who can handle being around others and working in groups.

YES   NO   MAYBE   I like meeting new people and I can be open to diverse beliefs and opinions.
- Much of military life is meeting new people, whether it is other servicemen and women or people in other countries and from other cultures. Flexibility and openness are important qualities in a service member. The military does not tolerate discrimination and service men and women are expected to be able to be tolerant of the people — both military and civilian — with whom they have to work.

YES   NO   MAYBE   I like to travel.
- You will travel if you join the military, but remember that you won't always get to choose where you will travel to. The military will try to station you in locations where you want to go, but the military's needs always come first.
- If you join the reserves or the National Guard (meaning you will be serving part-time, rather than on active duty which is full-time), then you will be assigned to a reserve unit in your area. This does not mean, however, that you won't travel. Reservists and National Guard members still travel for training or when they are called to war or to assist in relief operations.

YES   NO   MAYBE   I am a conscientious objector. I refuse to fight or participate in any war because of my religious, personal, moral, or ethical beliefs.

- Then you SHOULD NOT join the military. If you try to enlist, the recruiter will ask you if you are a conscientious objector. If you say yes, then you will ineligible for enlistment. If you lie, then you could face severe penalties later on if you object to being sent to war. The military is a fighting institution. It trains its members to fight, to wage war, and to kill. If any of these seem like they are something you cannot do with a clear conscience, then you should seek out other service options.

YES   NO   MAYBE   I am okay with some wars, but only if I agree with the government's reasons for waging them.

- The military exists to carry out government policy. Service personnel are expected to obey their superiors all the way up to the President of the United States, who is the Commander in Chief of the armed forces. Whether or not service members agree with those orders is immaterial. They still have to obey. While in the military you will retain your rights as a United States citizen and can use your vote to try to change government policy, but you will still be expected to fight in the wars waged by the United States until such time as that policy changes.

YES   NO   I have dependents.

- Dependents are any people that you have to take care of: your current spouse; any of your children or stepchildren who live with you or who you support, who are under 18, and unmarried; and any other family members who need you for more than half of their support. The branches of military limit the number of dependents that you can have because they require you to be able to adequately support them financially. Each branch has its own regulations about how many dependents you can have and whether or not having dependents will require you to get a waiver in order to enlist. Your recruiter can tell you more about the policies of his or her branch.

YES   NO   I am married.
- You can serve in the military while married, but you and your spouse should both know that military service can put a strain on your marriage. You may be away for long periods of time and face stresses that your spouse may not understand. You'll both have to work hard to make your marriage a success.
- If your spouse is already in the military, then you'll need to work with your recruiter and your superior officers to help you arrange to be assigned to duty stations near each other. You should also know that the military has strict policies on fraternization between officers and enlisted personnel, so if one of you is an officer and one is enlisted, this could cause problems during your time of service.

YES   NO   I am a single parent.
- The military will NOT allow you to enlist if you are a single parent with sole custody of one or more children. In order to enlist, you will have to give up custody of your child or children and then often wait several months to a year before being eligible to enlist. If you have joint custody of your child or children, then you will have to fully turn over custody to the other parent during the time in which you are in basic training. Additionally the other custodial parent will have to sign a statement agreeing to that arrangement before you are eligible to enlist.
- Those service members who become single parents while in the military find that single-parenting can often be incompatible with military service. The military requires that service personnel place their jobs before their families. They must be ready to deploy at a moment's notice and must have a local person who will sign a written agreement to take charge of their children with no prior notice. Any violation of a "Family Care Plan" will result in an immediate discharge.

YES   NO   MAYBE I am not married and I don't have kids, but I want to have a family someday.

- You can have a family and serve in the military. Many military service men and women are married and have children. Most military bases have childcare facilities, schools, playgrounds, and family housing. There are no longer any regulations preventing women from being pregnant while on active or reserve duty and there are even special pregnancy uniforms. And the tight-knit military community means a built-in support system for your family.
- However, raising a family while serving in the military has its own special challenges. You will likely be away from your family for extended periods of time, missing birthdays, anniversaries, and holidays. Your family will have to move often, usually every three to five years, which means your children will have to change schools and your spouse will need a career where he or she can change jobs often. Military pay, especially enlisted pay and especially for lower ranking enlisted personnel, is not high and it can be tough to make ends meet. And military work puts you at risk for stress, injury, illness, and death, so you will have to make sure that your family is prepared for any eventuality.

YES   NO   I am female.

- Today's military could not operate without its female soldiers, sailors, Airmen, Coast Guardsmen, and Marines. Women serve in all five branches as both officers and enlisted. With the exception of some adjustments for physical qualifications, women are held to the same standards as men when enlisting in the services. That said, though, there are some things that women who are interested in serving should consider.
- First of all, women in the Air Force, Army, Marine Corps, and Navy are not eligible for all jobs. Combat jobs are off-limits to female service members and women are not allowed to serve in

the Special Forces, such as the SEALs. (The Coast Guard, however, has no gender qualifications on any of its career fields.) The military's restrictions do not mean that women do not see combat, though. Military women are still sent to war zones such as Iraq and Afghanistan and their duties there, as well as the fluid nature of modern warfare, often mean that they see as much combat as their male comrades.

- Second, all potential enlistees need to consider any children they currently have and whether or not they are likely to have children in the future. Women — and men — are allowed to serve in the military while also being parents, but there are many challenges that come with those dual roles. Read the information above about dependents, single parents, and family life in the military.

- Finally, enlistees should know that rape and sexual assault, of both male and female personnel, is a problem in the military. In April 2011, fifteen female veterans and two male veterans brought a lawsuit against the Department of Defense, charging that military commanders did not do enough to prevent sexual assault, to support victims, and to prosecute offenders. According to the Service Women's Action Network, over 3000 military sexual assaults were reported in 2010, though the Pentagon estimates that 70–80 percent of military sexual assaults are unreported. The military has policies about sexual harassment and offenders who are found guilty of rape and assault are dealt with, but many victims say that they are reluctant to bring charges against their attacker or attackers for fear that they will not be believed or that it will adversely affect their careers. The Pentagon is looking into the situation, but at this time it remains a serious issue.

YES   NO   MAYBE   I am homosexual or bisexual.
- In December 2010, President Barack Obama signed a bill into law which overturned "Don't Ask, Don't Tell," the policy

which allowed homosexuals to serve in the military only if they did not tell anyone their sexual orientation or participate in homosexual activities (i.e., sex or gay marriage). Though there was much back and forth in court about overturning the policy, it was finally repealed officially on September 20, 2011. As of that date, men and women serving in the military can no longer be discharged for admitting that they are homosexual or bisexual and potential enlistees are no longer considered ineligible if they are gay. (Transgender persons were excluded from the repeal and transgender persons are not eligible to enlist if they have had a sex change operation.) Service personnel who were discharged under "Don't Ask, Don't Tell" will be allowed to reenlist if they desire.

- Even before the repeal of "Don't Ask, Don't Tell," homosexuals were serving in the military. Estimates say that over 70,000 homosexual men and women were serving in the military as of May 2010 and over a million veterans are gay, lesbian, or bisexual. The repeal is expected to bring in roughly 37,000 new homosexual and bisexual enlistees.

- But even with the repeal of "Don't Ask, Don't Tell," there will still be years of work to do in order to insure that gay service personnel are openly integrated into military life. The first men and women serving openly will likely face harassment, tension, stress, and more, just as the first minorities and the first women did when they integrated into the military, though the military branches are working to insure that troops are trained in the policy that sexual orientation has nothing to do with the military's mission. If you are homosexual or bisexual, you are allowed to enlist and serve, but you will probably have to work even harder to prove yourself during your time of service. At this time the Pentagon is not planning on adding sexual orientation to its equal opportunity policy, so you will probably not have a legal way to fight discrimination and harassment which is based on your orientation.

- Additionally, the Department of Defense (DoD) is restricted by the 1996 Defense of Marriage Act, which limits marriage to that of one man and one woman, so partners of gay service members will not be eligible for certain spousal benefits, such as on base housing or medical coverage. And if even if you are legally married in a state that allows gay marriage, the federal government does not acknowledge your marriage for purposes such as filing taxes or receiving death benefits, so the military cannot recognize your marriage either. However, the Pentagon has ruled that military chaplains are allowed, if they so choose, to perform wedding services for homosexual couples in states where gay marriage is legal. There are likely to be more changes as policies are enacted that address the issues of gay service members.

YES   NO   I am not a United States citizen.
- You can only join the military if you are a United States citizen or if you are a legal permanent resident who has a green card and is living in the United States. The military will not help you immigrate and cannot help your family immigrate after you join. If you have lived in a country that is considered hostile to the United States, then you will have to get a waiver in order to be able to enlist. Additionally, job opportunities for non-citizens are more limited as you will not be eligible for the security clearances needed for some jobs. Once non-citizens have enlisted, however, there are accelerated programs that will help them become citizens.

YES   NO   I am currently having financial or legal problems.
- The military is not a way for you to escape your financial or legal obligations. You will not be allowed to enlist until you have cleared up any financial or legal issues, such as bad credit or scheduled court appearances. Some financial or legal problems could also affect your choice of military jobs, since they could hinder your ability to get a security clearance.

YES NO   I have a criminal background or have had scrapes with the law in the past.

- You will need to talk with a recruiter about whether or not your past crimes will keep you from being eligible for military service. Criminal waivers are available in some cases, but the requirements vary depending upon the crime. All past brushes with the law will come to light during either the enlistment process or during a security clearance check, so you must not lie or omit information when talking to your recruiter.

YES NO   I have a physical disability or serious health issue.

- Depending upon what that disability or illness is you may be ineligible for military service. There is a very long list of disabilities and illnesses that will make you ineligible. Recruiters can give you the complete and up-to-date list, as well as tell you if you might qualify for a medical waiver which will allow you to serve despite your medical history.

YES NO   I am a drug user or have used drugs in the past.

- The military takes drug use very seriously. All service personnel are regularly tested for drug use. If you are thinking about enlisting and are currently using drugs, now is the time to get help and stop. You will not be able to continue using drugs while you are in the service. Even if all you use is tobacco, you will not have access to it during recruit training, so stopping now will make training easier for you.
- If you have used drugs in the past, even if you only experimented a single time, you will need to be honest about your usage when you talk with a recruiter. He or she can let you know if your drug use makes you ineligible for service or if you will need to apply for a medical or criminal waiver in order to enlist. This also goes for legal drugs which were prescribed for you by your doctor (such as Ritalin or antidepressants).

These are some of the things you should consider about your personality, your goals, and your past and present life. It is important to carefully consider all factors before making the decision to join the military. Think about your goals and whether or not a military career is compatible with them. If you want to learn a trade, does the military have jobs you can learn and then apply to a civilian career? Are you eligible for those jobs? What are the limitations on money you'll receive for education? How long will you have to enlist for? Consider all of the negatives and all of the positives of military service and decide if the negatives outweigh the positives for you. Now is the time to think clearly, rationally, and logically. Do your research and consider all options carefully.

2

Things to Consider
for Parents of
Potential Enlistees

If your son or daughter is considering joining the military, you will probably feel a mix of emotions. You may be proud that he or she is contemplating enlistment, especially if by doing so he or she is continuing a family tradition of military service. But you may also be worried. You may wonder if he or she will be tricked by a crafty recruiter. You may be concerned that your son or daughter may not be able to handle the rigors of basic training. You might fear for his or her life in facing the very real possibility of going to war or fighting. You may want him or her to do something different in life: go to college, get a civilian job, serve in another way. All of these feelings are normal and natural.

The most important thing to remember is that ultimately this is your child's decision. He or she must make the choice that is right for him or her. The military does not want enlistees who were coerced into joining and they don't want enlistees who haven't fully examined their reasons for enlisting. You and your child need to sit down together and discuss all of the options available to him or her. Calmly state your concerns and thoughts, but be sure that your child has enough time to say his or her piece. You need to know what he or she is thinking in order to help him or her make a decision. Here are some possible discussion questions:

- Why are you interested in joining the military?
- What other options are available to you? Can you go to school,

get a job, accept an apprenticeship, do mission work or service work for another agency, etc.?

- What opportunities does the military offer that you cannot get in college, in a private sector job, or in another service organization?
- What pros and cons do you see with military service? What will you gain and what will you have to give up with military service?
  - Go over Chapter 1: Things to Consider with your child to help answer these questions.
- Are you interested in being active duty or in joining the reserves?
  - Either way, he or she will still be gone for basic training and any follow on training. But after that training is over,

Proud parents hug their Coast Guard son (Official U.S. Coast Guard photograph by Petty Officer 3rd Class Tara Molle).

reservists return home and serve with a unit close to where they live, assuming there is a reserve unit near them.

- Are you thinking of doing just one tour of duty in the military or are you leaning towards making it a lifelong career?
  - o Even one tour of duty is about an eight-year commitment, accounting for both active duty time and time spent in the inactive reserves. More information can be found in Chapter 1.
- Which branch or branches of the military are you interested in? Why do they appeal to you? What do they offer that the other branches do not?
  - o Ideally potential enlistees will research all branches of the military before ever speaking to a recruiter, so that they will have an idea which branch or branches might be best suited to their interests and abilities. This book is specifically about the Coast Guard, but Chapter 5 has basic information about each branch and the other books in the series address the other branches.
- What job or jobs would you like to do in the military? Why is the military the best place to learn and practice that job or those jobs? Are there civilian opportunities to train and work in that field or those fields?
- Do you know anything about life in the military? What housing is available? What services are offered both on base and off? What hours will you work?
  - o Military life varies widely depending on if a service member is on base or off, on a ship or not, active duty or reservist, junior enlisted or senior, what job he or she is doing, etc. If you and your family have the time, take a tour of military bases from all branches. Approach the tour as you would a college tour — look over the facilities, talk to people who are living and working there, ask any questions you have. The public affairs personnel on base can help you schedule a tour.
- What benefits — health, medical, financial, educational — does the

military offer? What are the limitations attached to these benefits?

- Are you ready to deploy for months at a time if you are assigned to do so? Do you feel capable of dealing with the realities of war? Will you be able to fight and kill if told to do so?
- Have you spoken with any military personnel?
  - Help your child arrange to speak both with personnel serving right now and with retired personnel. Just remember that those who have retired will not have the most up-to-date information on benefits, jobs, life in the military, etc. But they will be able to tell your child how their service changed them for both good and ill.
- What are the enlistment requirements for each branch of the military? Do you meet those basic requirements?
  - Chapter 9 has the basic requirements for the Coast Guard.
- Do you feel academically ready to take the Armed Services Vocational Aptitude Battery (ASVAB) test? How can I help you prepare?
  - There is more information on the ASVAB in Chapter 13.
- Do you feel that you are in good enough physical shape for military training and service? Are you prepared to improve your physical fitness level so that you will be ready for basic training?
- Are you mentally ready to give up a lot of your personal freedom during your time in basic training and, to a lesser degree, while you are serving in the military?
- How will serving in the military affect your personal life? Is your boyfriend/girlfriend/husband/wife prepared for and supportive of you enlisting?
  - If your child is married, he or she should have his or her spouse look over Chapter 3: Things to Consider for Spouses.
- *If your child has children*: How will you support your children

while you are in the military? Is your spouse prepared to be a part-time single parent? *If your child is a single parent*: What are the military's regulations on enlisting as a single parent? What family care plan will you put in place while you are training and serving?

- o Many branches of the military will not allow single parents to enlist. Most require them to give up custody of their children before they are allowed to join. While serving, parents must have a family care plan in place so that their children do not affect their ability to do their military job, which includes being able to be deployed at short notice.
- If you are unable to join the military for any reason, what would you do instead?
- Can I come with you when you meet with recruiters?
  - o This will give you the opportunity to ask any questions or voice any concerns you might have. Remember, though, that your child's meetings with recruiters *must* be led by your child. He or she should do most of the talking and most of the responding to the recruiters' queries. You are only there in an advisory and supportive capacity. More information on meeting with recruiters can be found in Chapter 10.
  - o NOTE: if your child is 17, then you will have to come with him or her to recruiter meetings and you will have to give your permission before he or she can enlist.

Your child may not have all the answers to these questions at first. The questions are designed to help him or her spot areas where he or she needs to do more research. The best thing you can do is to help him or her find out more about all aspects of military service. Look at both the pros and cons of enlisting. For some people the military is a rewarding lifelong career. For others it is a time when they are paid to learn a trade, while also earning money for their education and while giving back to their country. And some other people discover that military service is not for them. Maybe they have physical issues which preclude service or maybe they decide that their skills, interests, and goals do not mesh with military life. No matter what your child decides, even taking the time to consider military service will teach him or her a lot about who he or she is inside and what his or her goals are for the future.

3

Things to Consider for Spouses of Potential Enlistees

There are a lot of reasons why your husband or wife might be considering joining the military. Perhaps he or she has finally decided to follow a childhood dream of enlisting. Maybe he or she feels a call to service that can no longer be denied. If the job market in your area is bad or if your spouse does not have the appropriate training, education, or skills for the available jobs, then the military might seem like a good option which will allow him or her to support your family. But whatever your spouse's reasons for enlisting, you both need to sit down and talk carefully about what joining the military will mean for your family. Look over the questions for potential enlistees in Chapter 1. The questions will give you an idea of some of the things you and your spouse need to think about when he or she considers enlistment. Here are some other possible discussion questions:

- What opportunities does the military offer our family that we cannot get by you going to college, getting a private sector job, or joining another service organization?
- What pros and cons do you see with military service? What will we as a family gain and what will we have to give up if you enlist in the military?
- Are you interested in being active duty or in joining the reserves?
  - Either way, he or she will still be gone for basic training and any follow on training. But after that training is over, reservists will return home and serve with a unit close

to where they live, assuming there is a reserve unit near them.

- Are you thinking of doing just one tour of duty in the military or are you leaning towards making it a lifelong career?
  - Know that even one tour of duty is about an eight year commitment, accounting for both active duty time and time spent in the inactive reserves. More information can be found in Chapter 1.
- Which branch or branches of the military are you interested in? Why do they appeal to you? What do they offer that the other branches do not?
  - Ideally potential enlistees will research all branches of the military before ever speaking to a recruiter, so that they will have an idea which branch or branches might be best suited to their interests and abilities. This book is specifically about the Coast Guard, but Chapter 5 has basic information about each branch and the other books in the series address the other branches.

Military marriages can be challenging, but there are many rewards as well (Official U.S. Marine Corps photograph by Lance Cpl. Daniel Boothe).

- What job or jobs would you like to do in the military? Why is the military the best place to learn and practice that job or those jobs? Are there civilian opportunities to be trained and work in that field or those fields?
- What are the enlistment requirements for each branch of the military? Do you meet those basic requirements?
  - Chapter 9 has the basic requirements for the Coast Guard.
- Do you feel academically ready to take the Armed Services Vocational Aptitude Battery (ASVAB) test? How can I help you prepare?
  - There is more information on the ASVAB in Chapter 13.
- Do you feel that you are in good enough physical shape for military training and service? Are you prepared to improve your physical fitness level so that you will be ready for basic training?
- *If you and your spouse have a child or children:* How will we support our child or children while you are in the military? What will it mean for me to be a part-time single parent while you are training or deployed? What family care plan will we need to put in place while you are training and serving?
- How will our family be taken care of in the event that you are injured or killed while training or deployed?
- What support services exist on base to help military spouses? Will I be left alone for long periods of time while you are gone? How will we keep our marriage strong while you are away?
- What is life in the military like? What housing is available? What services are offered both on base and off? What hours will you work?
  - Military life varies widely depending on if a service member is on base or off, on a ship or not, active duty or reservist, junior enlisted or senior, what job he or she is doing, etc. If you and your family have the time, take a tour of military bases from all branches — look over the facilities, talk to people who are living and working there, ask any questions you

have. The public affairs personnel on base can help you schedule a tour.
- What benefits — health, medical, financial, educational — does the military offer? What are the limitations attached to these benefits? Do they just cover the service member or do they cover his or her family as well?
  - See Chapter 4: Military Benefits for more information.
  - If you and your spouse/partner are a same-sex couple, you should know that at this time, the military does not offer many benefits to same-sex spouses/partners of military personnel.

These questions are a starting point for you and your spouse to be talking over the possibility of military service. They should help you both learn what areas you need to research further. As your spouse continues to look into the possibility of military service, help him or her. Go to the recruiters' offices with your spouse. (More information on visiting recruiters can be found in Chapter 10.) Help him or her study for the ASVAB and get in shape physically. Whether or not your spouse decides that military service is right for him or her, the journey into the enlistment process offers you the opportunity to learn more about each other and your goals and desires for the future.

Military Benefits

While military men and women give up a lot during their time in the service, they also receive benefits to help them out. Those benefits range from basic pay you receive for doing your job, to allowances for living expenses, to extras like educational benefits. The list of benefits is extensive and varies slightly by branch of service, years of service, job, and rank. You will never get rich working for the military, but the benefits you receive can, when used wisely, help you save money, get an education, and prepare for retirement and/or a civilian career. Your recruiter will have the most up-to-date information on benefits and during your time of service your commanding officers will keep you apprised of what benefits are available to you. There are several resources about military benefits listed in the "For More Information" section as well.

The major categories of military benefits afforded to service men and women are: pay, allowances, and incentives; vacation or leave time; housing and meal benefits; medical coverage; educational benefits; and more.

Pay, Allowances, and Incentives

Basic military pay is the same for all branches of the service, but varies by rank and years of service. An E-1 (the junior-most enlisted rank; a Seaman Recruit in the Coast Guard) with less than four months of active duty will make $1357.60 per month as of 2011, but as soon as he or she has over four months of active duty service, then pay will be $1467.60 per month. Enlisted service men and women who make it all the way to the top of the enlisted ranks (E-9, a Master Chief Petty Officer in the Coast Guard) make between $4600 and $5100 per month at this time. Military personnel are paid on the 1st and 15th of each month.

Military pay tables are available here: *http://www.dfas.mil/dfas/ militarymembers/payentitlements/militarypaytables.html*. Each year Congress decides whether or not to raise military pay. The latest military pay charts will be located at *http://www.dfas.mil* under the heading "Military Pay."

In addition to the basic pay, military service members receive allowances. Allowances help cover the cost of housing, uniforms, etc. Housing allowance is for military service members who decide to and are able to live off base. It is designed to help cover the cost of renting or buying a home. If you are stationed in an expensive part of the country or world, then you may qualify for a cost-of-living allowance in addition to the housing allowance. There is also a basic allowance for subsistence which helps cover the cost of food purchased off base. Your clothing allowance helps defray the cost of buying and maintaining your uniforms. After you are issued your initial uniform during basic training, you are given an allowance to help you replace parts of the uniform that have worn out or need updating. This allowance varies depending upon how long you have served in the military. There is also an allowance to help you cover the cost of military moves and an allowance you receive when you are assigned away from your family for a long period of time, usually longer than 30 days. Generally most allowances are not taxable, which means you do not owe the government money for them each year as you do with your pay.

Incentives are the broad range of special pay which some military personnel earn. Incentives may be given based on job, such as working on a submarine or working as a parachute jumper. There is incentive pay for military personnel on flying status and for those assigned on a ship at sea. You can earn incentive pay if you are a diver, if you are proficient in and work with a foreign language, if you are assigned to a foreign country, or if you are stationed away from your dependents for over 30 days and they cannot accompany you. Incentive pay is given for hazardous duty and for service in a combat zone. Additionally, if a military service member serves in a combat zone, then his or her pay received during that time may be exempt from Federal taxes.

Vacation or Leave Time

Military personnel do get time off and they earn vacation time — called "leave"—at a rate of 2½ days per month for a total of 30 days a year, but unlike in civilian jobs, when you are on vacation weekends are counted as part of your leave. However, you do not get to take your vacation whenever you would like. Your time off has to be approved by your supervisor and he or she can deny your request if the military decides they need you to keep working.

Housing Benefits

Most military bases have some form of housing available, but who can live there and whether or not there is room for everyone varies depending upon the size of the base, the location of the base, and other factors. Generally speaking, lower-rank (junior) enlisted personnel who are single must live on base in the barracks. These range from shared rooms with shared baths (much like a dorm room at a college) to small, apartment-like singles where you and another service member share living quarters, but have separate bedrooms and bathrooms. Living in the barracks not only means sharing, it also means you are subject to inspections (both announced and unannounced). If you are assigned to a ship for any reason, your living quarters will be much more basic. Ship's berths are generally communal, as are the bathrooms, and they are small, so be prepared to share.

Junior enlisted personnel are sometimes allowed live off base, but they will not receive a housing or food allowance, so it can be hard to afford it on their pay. As you rise up the enlisted ranks, you become

Sleeping quarters onboard ships can be small, but they still allow plenty of room for relaxing with friends (Official U.S. Coast Guard photograph by Petty Officer 1st Class NyxoLyno Cangemi).

eligible to live off base using a housing allowance to help you afford a place of your own.

Married service members can live on base in apartments, duplexes, or separate houses, depending upon what is available on base, what rank you are, and how big your family is. Families can also use their housing allowance to live off base. If you are married to another military member, things are a little trickier, especially if you are in different branches of the service. The military tries to station you together as best it can, but that "best" is usually considered to be at duty stations within 100 miles of each other. And even with the overturn of the "Don't Ask, Don't Tell" policy, gay service members and their partners/spouses are not eligible for married, on base housing.

Meal Benefits

When you live on base in the barracks or if you are assigned to a ship, then you will generally eat in the dining hall. You will receive a basic allowance for food, but most of that will go directly to the dining hall to pay for the meals you are supposed to receive. Personnel living off base or those in houses on base provide their own meals, though they also receive the subsistence allowance to help pay for food.

Medical Coverage

The military, like most employers, offers healthcare benefits to their personnel. Active duty personnel are completely covered for both medical and dental. Servicemen and women can also make sure their immediate family is covered as well, through the military's healthcare plan called Tricare. (Gay service members' partners/spouses are not eligible for coverage. Their biological or adopted children may be eligible, but stepchildren will not be.) Tricare has several different types of coverage. In some of those plans, immediate family members of active duty personnel are completely covered without any extra costs, but with some limitations, while other plans have a yearly deductible. Reserve military personnel are covered during the time they are on active duty, and they can purchase coverage for their family during those times, but otherwise they are not covered. Military retirees no longer get free medical care for life, as they were promised in the past, but they can still belong to Tricare. Your recruiter will have the most up-to-date information on healthcare costs or more information on Tricare can be found at *http:// www.tricare.mil.*

Educational Benefits

Many people join the military because of the education benefits. In addition to the job training all military personnel receive, they also have access to programs which can help them earn a college degree, either while serving or afterwards. Through distance education programs, many military personnel can work towards a degree during their off-duty hours, though you should be aware that earning a degree this way takes longer than going to school full-time and in the military it can sometimes be hard to find off-duty time for classwork, depending on what your job is. Bases and ships often offer classes to their personnel, providing the space for professors and students to work. All of the military branches also offer tuition assistance which will cover the cost of classes and fees, though there are limitations on how much they will reimburse you per semester hour (generally around $250) and a cap on yearly reimbursements (generally $4,500).

The most well-known education benefit is probably the GI Bill. There are several variants of the GI Bill, but all new military enlistees are automatically enrolled in what is called the Post–9/11 GI Bill. This new version of the bill adds to and adapts the benefits offered, but still with the goal of helping military service members pay for college. You will usually use your benefits after you leave or retire from the military, though you can also use your benefits while on active duty or in the reserves. The Department of Veterans Affairs, better known as the Veterans Administration (VA), pays your GI Bill benefits directly to your college or university and also offers a stipend of up to $1000 per year to help you cover the cost of books. Veterans and reservists also qualify for a monthly housing stipend as long as they are attending school full-time and not using a distance education program. One new benefit with the Post–9/11 GI Bill is the ability for personnel who have served in the military for at least ten years to transfer their GI Bill benefits to their spouses or children. GI Bill benefits are limited to 36 months and must be used within 15 years of leaving active duty service. You must have been discharged from the service honorably in order to receive GI Bill benefits.

You do not have to be planning to go to a two- or four-year college to use your GI Bill benefits. The benefits also cover you if you are planning on taking a correspondence course, receiving flight training, participating in a non-college degree program (such as beauty school or truck driver training), accepting an apprenticeship, or doing on-the-job training (as in police academy training or plumbing). Your benefits can help you pay for training and can offer you supplemental income as you work your way to a new career.

The VA also has a program to support the children and spouses of military personnel who were killed in action or permanently disabled. It is called Survivors and Dependents Assistance. You can receive this benefit even if you are military yourself and it can be combined with the GI Bill benefits to give you up to 45 months of educational support. It cannot, however, be used for correspondence course training.

Additionally every branch except the Air Force has a type of college fund. These funds, sometimes referred to as a "GI Bill Kicker," are in addition to the amount that you will receive through the GI Bill. The amounts you hear mentioned in ads for the military (i.e. "$40,000 for college") are the amount you will receive through the GI Bill added to the amount you will receive from the college fund. You cannot receive the college fund without getting the GI Bill, but with the college funds it is the military branches, not the Veterans Administration, that decide who is eligible.

Other Benefits

There are a wide variety of other benefits open to military personnel. Bases often have "commissaries" (grocery stores) and "exchanges" (department stores) for personnel and their families to shop. These facilities are on base, do not charge sales tax, and usually have slightly lower prices than comparable stores in town, which can save you and your family some money and time when you are picking up essentials, though the selection can be limited depending upon the size of your base. Morale, Welfare, and Recreation services are available for personnel and their families and they include recreation centers (which offer everything from discount tickets to shows and attractions to classes to family fun programs), gymnasiums for keeping fit, child development centers for families where both parents work full-time, libraries, and more. And if you serve active duty for twenty years, then you can retire with most military benefits and military retirement pay.

The Branches of
the Military

If you decide that a military career might be a good fit for you, you'll then need to decide which branch of the service you might be interested in. You should to talk to recruiters from all branches of the service, even if you think you know which branch you want to join. They can give you an idea of what their branch has to offer, tell you about how their branch is structured and what the enlistment requirements and expectations are, and help you to find out if their branch is good fit for you in terms of its culture and its job offerings.

Which Branch to Join?

This volume focuses specifically on the Coast Guard, but before going into detail about the Coast Guard, we'll look at all of the branches of the military in general, each separately covered in the companion books. There are five branches of the military: the Army, the Navy, the Air Force, the Marine Corps, and the Coast Guard, from largest to smallest.

ARMY

The United States Army is the oldest of the United States' military branches, founded in June 1775, and also the largest. Its main job is to fight on land using ground troops, tanks, helicopters, artillery, etc. As of September 2010 there were 561,378 people serving on active duty in the Army (not counting cadets at the United States

Military Academy): 94,128 officers and 467,248 enlisted. Of those numbers, 15,070 of the officers were female and 60,377 of the enlisted personnel were female, about 13 percent of the Army's force. The Army also has two reserve units: the Army Reserve, which is run by the federal government, and the Army National Guard. Each state maintains its own National Guard units, rather than them being controlled by the national government. In 2009, there were 645,394 personnel total in the Army Reserves and the Army National Guard.

Army Emblem (United States Army).

NAVY

The United States Navy was also founded in the summer of 1775, though it was disbanded after the Revolutionary War and not officially reinstated until 1794. The Navy is the United States' sea-based branch of the military. Its mission is to fight battles at sea using ships and submarines. The Navy

Navy Seal (United States Navy).

works closely with the United States Marine Corps to accomplish that mission. The Navy also uses its large aircraft carriers to launch air attacks and can launch land attacks using long-range missiles. In April 2011 323,745 personnel — 52,364 officers and 271,381 enlisted — were serving on active duty in the Navy (not counting midshipmen at the United States Naval Academy), with 8,184 female officers and 43,438 female enlisted personnel or almost 16 percent of the Navy. The Navy does have a Reserve component and 109,271 personnel were serving in the Navy Reserve in 2009.

AIR FORCE

The United States Air Force is the youngest branch of the military, formed after World War II by the National Security Act of 1947. It is the aviation branch of the military and uses its resources to defend the United States in the air and in space. It has a wide variety of aircraft for fighting, transport, bombing, rescue, etc. The Air Force is also responsible for all military satellites. In September 2010, 329,638 service men and women were active duty in the Air Force (not counting cadets at the United States Air Force Academy), with 66,201 officers and 263,437 enlisted. Women made up 19 percent of those numbers, with 12,363 women serving as officers and 50,946 women serving as enlisted. The Air Force has a Reserve component and there are Air National Guard units in each state. In 2009 there were 220,364 personnel serving in both.

Air Force Seal (United States Air Force).

MARINE CORPS

The United States Marine Corps started during the Revolutionary War, but wasn't officially established as a separate branch until 1798. The Marine Corps is closely connected with the United States Navy. The Marine Corps' mission of amphibious warfare — launching land attacks from sea — is a good complement to the Navy's sea-based mission. The Marines also train forces in ground combat and use aircraft and helicopters to attack. They use the Navy for medical support and some administrative support. The Marines are a small service, with about 201,623 people serving on active duty in September 2010. At that time there were 21,307 officers and 181,134 enlisted, about 7.5 percent of which were female (3,054 officers and 12,203 enlisted). There is a Marine Corps Reserve, comprised of 95,199 personnel in 2009.

Marine Corps Seal (United States Marine Corps).

COAST GUARD

The Coast Guard, which began as the Revenue Cutter Service in 1790, plays a unique role in the United States military. They handle boating safety, law enforcement, search and rescue, and other tasks related to maritime security. Unlike the other branches of the military, which operate under the Department of Defense, the Coast Guard is part of the Department of Homeland Security, though during times of war control of the Coast Guard can be transferred to the Navy, if so ordered by the President. In September 2010 the Coast Guard had 42,358 personnel on active duty: 8,508 officers and 32,837 enlisted, not counting cadets at the United States Coast Guard Academy. 5,552, or 13 percent, of these active duty personnel were women. There is a Coast Guard Reserve (with 9,399 personnel in 2009) and a volunteer, unpaid Coast Guard Auxiliary.

Coast Guard Seal (United States Coast Guard).

Even if you are positive that you only want to serve in the Coast Guard, it is to your benefit for you to learn about each of the branches of the military. The different branches do not operate completely independently and if you decide to enlist in the Coast Guard it is very likely that you will find yourself working with service members from other branches.

Next, in Part Two, we'll talk more specifically about the Coast Guard, looking at its history as well as what career opportunities are available for you in the Coast Guard.

Two

General Information About the Coast Guard

The History
of the Coast Guard

As long as there have been ships around the lands that are now the United States, there has been a need for people to monitor those ships and to rescue people in need on the water. That is the mission of the Coast Guard, though it was originally started for a very different reason.

Early Beginnings

After the Revolutionary War, the new United States government needed a way to collect revenue (or taxes) on goods being brought into the country and it also needed a way to prevent smuggling and piracy. In 1790, Alexander Hamilton, who was then Secretary of the Treasury, suggested that boats be built for that purpose. Congress agreed and ten boats — with forty officers and enlisted men — were built. At the time there was no Navy, so the new Revenue Service (called the Revenue Marine, but renamed the Revenue Cutter Service in 1894) was the only armed American seagoing service for eight years. Its early dual mission of both maritime law enforcement and protection of life and property at sea set the stage for some of the major roles of the future Coast Guard.

The United States Navy was re-established in 1798 to combat two problems: Barbary pirates who were capturing American merchant vessels and an undeclared war with France from 1798 to 1800. The Revenue Marine worked with the Navy on both issues, setting another tradition of having the Revenue Service (and later the Coast Guard) placed under the Navy's command in times of war or national emergency. The Revenue Service saw its first combat experience during this time, capturing fifteen French vessels. The Revenue Marine also saw action against the British during the War of 1812. A cutter seized the first British ship to be captured during the war, which lasted from 1812 to 1815.

Taxation and piracy remained the Revenue Service's primary missions for several more years, leading in some cases to armed conflicts. In a move that foreshadowed the coming Civil War, South Carolina voted in 1832 to nullify federal taxes, refusing to collect money on goods being imported. The Revenue Marine was ordered to sail five cutters into the harbor at Charleston to stop vessels coming in and to collect the taxes on their goods. During the early to mid–1800s, cutters also fought pirates operating out of New Orleans and the Caribbean, capturing their vessels and seizing contraband. Cutters were also assigned the task of preventing slave trading ships from entering the United States after Congress banned the importation of slaves.

Growth During the Mid–1800s

The duties of the Service gradually began to be expanded beyond war and taxes. In 1831, the Service was assigned to begin winter cruises in which they would aid ships in distress. This only lasted for one year, but in 1837 Congress authorized the use of Revenue Service vessels to cruise the coastline and help seafarers as needed. Lighthouses began to be more fully funded by Congress in 1848. These were often staffed by volunteers, both men and women. In areas where lighthouses were not practical, government lightships were positioned at regular intervals. Cutters began to modernize to steam-powered vessels in the 1840s, just as the government was beginning to see the need for official inspections to prevent poorly operated steamboats from causing disasters on United States waterways. Early environmental protection duties included protecting public lands from illegal logging.

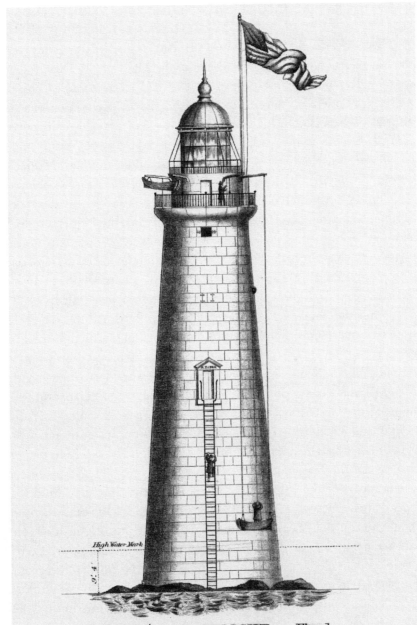

High Water Mark

9'4"

MINOT'S LEDGE LIGHT   Fixed
Height of Focal plane above mean high water 84 f. 7 ".

Minot's Ledge Lighthouse in 1861 (U.S. Coast Guard).

51

War was never far away, however. Cutters assisted the Army and the Navy during the Seminole War in Florida. The Treasury Department set up a Revenue Marine Bureau in 1843 and its new head, Captain Alexander Fraser, led reforms to make the Service perform on a more military-like basis. The Mexican War (1846–1848), fought mainly over control of some of the lands in the American Southwest, was a land-based war, but the Service assisted by blockading ports on Mexico's coasts. During the Civil War (1861–1865), the Revenue Service assisted the Union Navy with blockades of Southern ports and it helped protect northern shipping. The cutter *Harriet Lane*—which fired the first formal shot of the war across the bow of the CSS *Nashville*—was part of the first Union victories against Forts Clark and Hatteras in North Carolina. The *Harriet Lane* was captured in 1863 during a battle with the Confederate Army and Navy. Almost all crewmembers were killed.

After the Civil War, the Revenue Service returned to expanding its duties and responsibilities, with a renewed emphasis on training and rescue. The Revenue Service School of Instruction began on board a training ship in 1876. (The school moved to New London, Connecticut, in 1918 and became the Coast Guard Academy.) The government founded the United States Lifesaving Service in 1871, taking over the lighthouses it had helped build beginning in 1848 and assisting passengers of ships that had wrecked or were sinking. The Revenue Cutter Service ran the Lifesaving Service until 1878 when the LSS became a separate part of the Department of the Treasury. One hero from the Lifesaving Service was Captain Richard Etheridge, an African American man who ran the Pea Island Life Saving Station starting in 1880. He and his men, many of whom were also African American, gained a reputation for running one of the best stations on the North Carolina coast. He died while trying to save a life on May 8, 1900, but was not posthumously awarded a Gold Life Saving Medal for heroism until 1996. Women were also an important part of the Lifesaving Service. Ida Lewis-Wilson, who saved eighteen lives during her time as keeper of the Lime Rock Lighthouse in Newport, Rhode Island, was awarded a Gold Life Saving Medal in 1881 for her heroism.

Captain Richard Etheridge and his crew sometime around 1896 (U.S. Coast Guard).

In the late 1800s the Revenue Cutter Service began moving into the northern regions of the Earth. The Bering Sea Patrol, started in 1880, helped rescue whaling ships caught in ice, provided medical aid to the Eskimo peoples, protected sea life and even assisted scientists in reaching the arctic for scientific research purposes. Captain Michael A. Healy (son of an Irish immigrant and a mixed race slave) was the only African American to be commissioned in any of the services that later became the Coast Guard. He served much of his illustrious career in the waters off the Alaskan coast. His boat guarded against sealing, brought aid to native peoples, transported supplies, made weather reports, and imported reindeer herds to the Alaskan wilderness. The Revenue Cutter Service also journeyed into warmer climes when it assisted the other branches of the military during the Spanish-American War (1898). Some cutters helped blockade Havana, Cuba, and others were sent to the Pacific to participate in the Battle of Manila Bay in the Philippines.

Valor in the Early to Mid–1900s

In the early years of the twentieth century, the loss of vessels in collisions with icebergs in the North Atlantic — most famously, the *Titanic* disaster of 1912 — resulted in the formation of the International Ice Patrol. United States Revenue cutters led the patrol, with financial support from other nations. Furthering the Revenue Cutter Service's role as a life-saving organization, in 1915 President Woodrow Wilson signed a law combining the Revenue Cutter Service and the United States Lifesaving Service, along with the Steamship Inspection Bureau, into one organization called the Coast Guard. The new Coast Guard operated under the Treasury Department in times of peace, but was considered to be a branch of the military, responsible to the Navy in times of war.

That time of war came soon thereafter with the United States' 1917 entry into World War I (1914 to 1918). Coast Guard ships were given the task of policing all of the shipping traffic coming through American ports. They also escorted cargo ships and rescued survivors from damaged ships. One cutter, the *Tampa*, was destroyed — probably by a German U-boat — in 1918, killing all 111 Coast Guardsmen and four Navy men on board. African Americans were not officially admitted into the new Coast Guard during World War I, though there were African American men serving in the Lifesaving Service when it combined with the Revenue Cutter Service. During the same time period, women gradually began to enter the service. In 1918, twin sisters Genevieve and Lucille Baker became the first women to serve in uniform in the Coast Guard.

During the 1920s, the Coast Guard began experimenting with

adding airplanes to its fleet. Planes proved useful for search and rescue operations, but they were also used for policing the waters off the coast of the United States during Prohibition. In 1919 Congress passed the 18th Amendment banning the manufacture, transport, and sale of alcohol in the United States. Smuggling rings soon cropped up, trying to bring in alcohol from other countries. Coast Guard planes and ships were part of the government's front-line defense against these smugglers until the ban was repealed in 1933.

As the United States began to prepare for war with Germany and Japan, the Coast Guard was expanded once again when the Lighthouse Service was added to it in 1939. In 1941, the Navy once again took the reins of the Coast Guard when the United States was about to enter

The crew of the Coast Guard Cutter *Spencer* watch as the Nazi U-Boat they were fighting is destroyed (U.S. Coast Guard).

World War II (1939–1945). During the war, Coast Guard ships were an important part of the war effort. Crews chased submarines, escorted convoys, stowed dangerous explosives, protected vessels and ports, furnished weather reports, rescued survivors, staffed Navy and Army vessels, and took part in every major Pacific and European amphibious campaign, including the invasion of Normandy. Assisting the active-duty Coast Guard were two newly formed Reserve units. The Coast Guard Auxiliary, an all-volunteer force whose members are not paid for their work, was founded in 1939 and the Coast Guard Reserve was founded in 1941.

World War II was a time of important changes and firsts for the Coast Guard. The first American naval capture of the war was made by the *Northland* when her crew seized a German trawler in 1941. The *Sea Cloud* became the first racially integrated vessel in a United States naval service in 1943 and the first landing of a helicopter on board a ship occurred on the *Cobb* in 1944. The Bureau of Marine Inspection was added to the Coast Guard in 1942, bringing the Coast Guard to its current administrative configuration. Women were admitted into the Coast Guard Reserve in 1942 as part of the SPARs, doing administrative work.

Changes During the 1950s Through the 1980s

The Coast Guard returned to doing search-and-rescue and maritime law enforcement after World War II was over. In 1948, Congress gave them the responsibility for operating Long Range Navigation (LORAN), a system of electronic navigation aids. New high-endurance cutters began covering the Atlantic and Pacific Oceans. During the 1950s, the Coast Guard's enforcement of the Treasury Department's order to withhold licenses from merchant sailors who were considered "subversive" or suspected of Communist activity cast a dark shadow over the Guard. But focus on scientific exploration was a bright spot. Three Coast Guard cutters sailed through the Northwest Passage — a deep water passage north of North America — in 1957, proving that it was possible for merchant ships to pass through.

During the same period dramatic changes began within the military's ranks. The Women's Armed Services Integration Act of 1948 allowed women permanent status in the regular and reserve forces of the other military branches, though in the Coast Guard they were limited to the reserves only and there were restrictions on numbers and promotion levels which continued until 1967. Executive Order 9981 was also drafted in 1948, ending racial segregation in the military. African Americans had already served in the Coast Guard during World War II, including on an integrated ship and as officers, but by the time of the Vietnam War the Coast Guard was utilizing African American Coast Guardsmen in every capacity. In 1949 the Career Compensation Act was passed, bringing Coast Guard pay up to the same pay grades as the other services. And by 1967, the Coast Guard had been moved from the Treasury Department to the newly created Department of Transportation.

The Vietnam War (1965–1972) was a conflict between forces in South Vietnam and those in North Vietnam, which were supported by the Soviet Union and China, as well as the Viet Cong rebels in South Vietnam. During that time the Coast Guard sent squadrons to patrol the coastal waters of South Vietnam. Cutters kept the North Vietnamese forces from getting supplies to the Viet Cong rebels in the South. More than 8,000 Coast Guardsmen took part in the Vietnam War effort, on more than 50 Coast Guard vessels. After returning from Vietnam, the Coast Guard assisted with the Mariel Boatlift out of Cuba. Dictator Fidel Castro said that anyone could leave Cuba, but they had to do so through the tiny port at Mariel. Refugees fled on anything that could float. The Coast Guard and Navy were responsible for helping with the rescue effort.

During the late 1970s through the 1990s, the Coast Guard and the other military branches found themselves in a period of societal change. The draft was ended in 1973 and the military became an all-volunteer service. The SPARs program was ended in 1974 as women became full

Coast Guard cutters leave the Philippines bound for Vietnam in 1965 (U.S. Coast Guard).

members of the Coast Guard. In 1975 Congress passed Public Law 94–106, forcing the military academies to admit women. The Coast Guard Academy was the first to accept female applicants. By 1978, all Coast Guard career fields and enlisted ratings were open to both sexes. Lieutenant Junior Grade Beverly Kelly became the first woman to command a United States naval vessel when she took command of the patrol boat *Cape Newagen* in 1988.

Environmental protection has been part of the Coast Guard's mission for many years. In 1972, as part of the Ports and Waterways Act, the Coast Guard was put in charge of developing regulations for the construction of ships carrying polluting substances through United States waterways. They were also charged with developing systems to control vehicle traffic through crowded harbors to prevent accidents. When the U.S. tanker *Exxon Valdez* struck a reef off the coast of Alaska in 1989, spilling eleven million gallons of crude oil into Prince William Sound, the Coast Guard headed the clean-up effort.

The 1990s and On into a New Century

The Coast Guard continues to assist the other branches of the military during times of war. In August 1990, Iraq invaded its neighbor Kuwait, leading to the first Persian Gulf War in January 1991. The Coast Guard worked with the United States Navy in the Red Sea and Persian Gulf, patrolling, boarding ships, securing the blockade of Iraq, confiscating cargo, etc. Iraqi dictator Saddam Hussein ordered his men to commit sabotage by pouring oil from a Kuwaiti storage facility into the Persian Gulf and setting fire to several oil refineries. The Coast Guard worked with the United States Army, Navy, Environmental Protection Agency, and National Oceanic and Atmospheric Administration to put out the fires and clean up the damage. The Coast Guard also participated in the controversial boarding of a Russian commercial vessel accused of spying in 1997, several rescue efforts after hurricanes damaged Nicaragua and Honduras in 1998, and the conflict in Kosovo in 1999. The 1990s also saw the expansion of the Coast Guard's role in the drug war, as sharpshooters were placed in Coast Guard helicopters to compel suspected drug smuggling ships to stop and allow boarding.

Following the terrorist attacks of September 11, 2001, the Coast Guard added a new mission: homeland security. When the new Department of Homeland Security was formed in 2003, the Coast Guard moved under their control from the Department of Transportation. Reservists were called up to support active duty troops as the Coast Guard increased patrols around the United States and helped the Navy with overseas escort missions. Coast Guard personnel were responsible for reopening ports in New York and Baltimore, assisting emergency response agencies with clean-up and rescue efforts, and even providing counseling for firefighters, police and others. On October 7, 2001, the United States military began a campaign in Afghanistan against Al-Qaida and Taliban forces, leading to the overthrow of the Taliban government. The Coast Guard's efforts to secure the United States against terrorist threats directly supports the war in Afghanistan.

In the second Persian Gulf War, which began in 2003, United States forces fought alongside coalition forces to bring about the fall of the capital of Baghdad, leading to the end of the rule of Iraqi dictator Saddam Hussein and his Baath party in 2003. The Coast Guard deployed ships and personnel into the Persian Gulf in support of operations. In addition to patrolling, escorting craft, and boarding ships to search for contraband, the Coast Guard developed maps and instructions for passing through the war zone, searched for and cleared under-

Crew from a Coast Guard cutter help rescue illegal immigrants on an overcrowded and disabled boat (U.S. Coast Guard).

water mines, and prepared responses to possible pollution disasters, such as happened in the first Gulf War.

Another Coast Guard mission is the enforcement of immigration laws. From 1992 through 1994, the Coast Guard had to stop nearly 100,000 immigrants from entering the United States illegally as they fled the dictatorships of Cuba and Haiti. After 9/11, the Coast Guard was under even greater pressure to round up people in the United States illegally. Illegal immigration continues today, with most of the immigrants picked up by the Coast Guard fleeing from Haiti, the Dominican Republic, Cuba, China, and Mexico.

In addition to its focus on homeland security, counter-terrorism, the war on drugs, and illegal immigration, the Coast Guard is also still concerned with environmental protection. On April 20, 2010, a deepwater oil rig in the Gulf of Mexico exploded, resulting in an oil gusher that leaked hundreds of millions of gallons of oil into the Gulf. The Coast Guard assisted with clean-up and capping efforts, trying to restore the Gulf to its original state.

Today the Coast Guard continues to work with other military personnel and civilians to help keep our waterways safe and clean, to rescue those who need help at sea, and to prevent crime.

Career Opportunities
in the Coast Guard

Obviously one of the most important things you should consider when you begin thinking about which branch of the military you might want to enlist in is what jobs will be available to you in each branch. The recruiters you visit will help you learn about the career fields available in each branch, but you will be better off if you do some research before you enlist. That way you will know which job fields appeal to you and be able to make the decision that is right for your future.

What if you already know exactly what military career field you want to be in? You should still look at everything that is available. Many factors can prevent you from entering a particular field — the military may have too many people already doing that job, your test scores may show that the job is not a good fit for you, that job may not be open when you are ready to begin training, or the job may have restrictions which you cannot get around. If you have already looked at all the jobs available in each branch, then you can decide if you want to try for another job or if another branch may offer you a better change to achieve your dream.

What if you don't know what military career field you are interested in? Reading over all of the options available in each branch might give you some ideas, but your recruiter can help also. The Armed Services Vocational Aptitude Battery (ASVAB) test that you take during enlistment will show you and your recruiter what career fields you are best suited for. (We'll talk more about the ASVAB testing process in Part Three.) Each branch of the military will also have jobs that they are eager to fill. Your recruiter can tell you what those are and if you are qualified. So if you truly don't care what job you do, then you can allow yourself to be placed in one.

The type of job you want to do might depend upon whether you want to work in a hands-on field or a field where you are dealing with abstract concepts like information, numbers, or words. You also want to think about whether you prefer primarily working with machines or primarily working with people. Do you want to be in an exciting, ever-changing, possibly dangerous career or do you think you'd rather have a job with more stability? Are you more of a science and math oriented person or more of an arts and letters oriented person? These are all things to keep in mind as you consider the types of jobs the different military branches have to offer.

Unlike the other four branches of the military, the Coast Guard has no gender restrictions with its jobs. Women are allowed in every rating, as long as they meet the qualifications. (There is one exception: Coast Guardsmen are allowed to apply to become Navy SEALS while still retaining their status as active duty Coast Guard. This option is not available to women.) Some jobs are not open to enlistees who will be going into the reserves, however. Those jobs may only be filled by active-duty personnel. Your recruiter can tell you which jobs are open to you based on your test scores and whether you are going active duty or reserves.

Whatever career field you pick in whichever branch of the military, you will be working in that career field for at least the next four to eight years, so it is in your best interest to pick something that you think you will enjoy. If you enlist, the military is going to spend a lot of time and money training you, so it wants you to be in a job where you will work hard and excel. In Part Three you will learn about talking with your recruiter about your job possibilities. For now, let's look at what jobs are available in the Coast Guard.

Coast Guard Enlisted Careers

The Coast Guard is the smallest branch of the military, so it has the fewest jobs. But the jobs offered still have plenty of variety, so there is something for everyone who is interested in becoming a Guardian. Coast Guard jobs are broken into four groups: Deck and Ordnance, Hull and Engineering, Aviation, and Administrative and Scientific.

- Deck and Ordnance Group: Coast Guardsmen working in these jobs are responsible for operating all Coast Guard vessels.
- Hull and Engineering Group: Coast Guardsmen working in these jobs are responsible for maintenance and upkeep of all Coast Guard vessels.
- Aviation Group: Coast Guardsmen working in these jobs are all of the personnel, except for pilots, responsible for the operation and maintenance of Coast Guard aircraft.
- Administration and Scientific Group: Coast Guardsmen working in these jobs are responsible for supporting their fellow Coast Guardsmen and taking care of the environment.

Within these four groups are nineteen different jobs open to Coast Guard enlisted personnel.

Deck and Ordnance Group Ratings

- Boatswain's Mates: These Coast Guardsmen are responsible for many tasks on board vessels. They supervise deck personnel and can also work on any job related to deck maintenance. They also handle navigation and the operation of small craft.
- Gunner's Mates: These Coast Guardsmen are the weapons experts on board vessels.
- Intelligence Specialists: These Coast Guardsmen analyze communication signals, photos, maps, and other data to gather information relevant to the Coast Guard's missions and then report on their findings to other crewmembers.
- Maritime Enforcement Specialists: These Coast Guardsmen are the law enforcement professionals on board vessels. They handle port

A gunner's mate loads a test round into a 57mm gun onboard a cutter (Official U.S. Coast Guard photograph by Petty Officer 3rd Class Michael Anderson).

security and safety, enforce maritime laws, and act as an anti-terrorism force.

- Operations Specialists: These Coast Guardsmen are the ones who are in charge of coordinating Coast Guard missions, whether they are running a search-and-rescue operation or working on a homeland security task.

HULL AND ENGINEERING GROUP RATINGS

- Damage Controlmen: These Coast Guardsmen are responsible for maintenance of Coast Guard vessels, as well as emergency repairs.
- Electrician's Mates: These Coast Guardsmen install, maintain, and repair the electrical systems that power the Coast Guard's vessels and facilities.

Damage controlmen must repair the ship even while it is at sea (Official U.S. Coast Guard photograph by Petty Officer 3rd Class Thomas M. Blue).

- Electronics Technicians: These Coast Guardsmen keep sophisticated and specialized equipment — such as radar, navigation equipment, and command and control systems — running smoothly.
- Information System Technicians: These Coast Guardsmen are responsible for the Coast Guard's computer networks and telephones (analog and digital). They install, maintain, and repair those systems.
- Machinery Technicians: These Coast Guardsmen are in charge of many different aspects of repair, from engines to hydraulics to heating and air conditioning. They also handle some aspects of hazardous material recovery.

Aviation Group Ratings

- Avionics Electrical Technicians: These Coast Guardsmen are charged with repairing and maintaining many aircraft systems,

Aviation survival technicians trained as rescue swimmers are responsible for saving lives at sea (Official U.S. Coast Guard photograph by PA1 Donnie Brzuska, PADET Jacksonville, FL).

including communications, targeting, navigation, power generation, landing gear, anti-ice, fire control, hydraulics, automatic pilot controls, and more.

- Aviation Maintenance Technicians: These Coast Guardsmen repair and maintain many aircraft components, including wings, rotor blades, flight control surfaces, rotor systems, engines, and more. They also act as aircrew members, such as flight engineers, flight mechanics, loadmaster, etc.
- Aviation Survival Technicians: These Coast Guardsmen are helicopter rescue swimmers and emergency medical technicians. They also maintain survival equipment and train their fellow Coast Guardsmen in survival techniques.

ADMINISTRATIVE AND SCIENTIFIC GROUP RATINGS

- Food Services Specialists: These are the Coast Guardsmen who feed the rest of the Coast Guard. They not only cook, but they also manage the Coast Guard's food services facilities.
- Health Services Technicians: These are the Coast Guardsmen who keep the Coast Guard healthy. They provide both routine and emergency care, assist doctors and dentists, work in medical laboratories, help with surgery, prescribe medicine, and perform diagnostic tests.
- Marine Science Technicians: These Coast Guardsmen are directly responsible for environmental safety. They inspect vessels, ports, and containers and respond to oil and hazardous materials spills as well as natural disasters.
- Public Affairs Specialists: These Coast Guardsmen communicate with the public by writing news articles, taking pictures, making films, running websites, and acting as the Coast Guard's spokespersons.
- Storekeepers: These Coast Guardsmen are in charge of all aspects of buying, storing, and issuing supplies. They also keep the Coast Guard's financial records.

Marine science technicians inspect containers of hazardous waste (Official U.S. Coast Guard photograph by Petty Officer 3rd Class Melissa Hauck).

- Yeomen: These Coast Guardsmen are human resources personnel, assisting, advising, and keeping track of their fellow Coast Guardsmen and their dependents.

Whatever your interests, there is a Coast Guard career that might be a good fit for you. The next step is to talk to a recruiter. Part Three will give you all the tips you need to know to begin the enlistment process.

THREE

The Enlistment Process

What Is the Enlistment Process?

The enlistment process is the steps that take you from civilian to military recruit. It is an important process, filled with decisions that need to be considered soberly and at length. The choices you make during the enlistment process will shape your life for at least the next eight years and should shape the rest of your life, assuming you take full advantage of the training and educational opportunities afforded you during your military service. That means that you need to think carefully about all the options presented to you. You will receive a lot of information and advice from the recruiters you speak to, from your friends and family, and from research you do yourself. It is your job to compile all of that information and advice into a complete picture of what your options are. Until you give the Oath of Enlistment as you are leaving for basic training you are not obligated to anything, so take your time and make the decision that is right for you.

There aren't clearly defined steps that make up the enlistment process, since the experience is different for every recruit and the process varies depending upon which branch of the service you choose to enter. But there is a rough outline that each enlistment process will follow:

- Researching the different branches of the service and getting a general idea of what they are like
- Speaking with recruiters from all branches of the service
- Deciding which branch you are most interested in
- Completing paperwork detailing your past medical, legal, finan-

cial, and academic history to make sure that nothing in your past would prevent you from enlisting

- Taking the Armed Services Vocational Aptitude Battery test (the ASVAB) to see if you are qualified for that branch and to see which jobs you qualify for
- Visiting a Military Entrance Processing Station (MEPS) to get your physical
- Resolving any final physical, moral, or other waivers needed before being accepted into your chosen branch
- Taking the oath to enter the Delayed Entry Program
- Using your time in the Delayed Entry Program to get into physical and mental shape before basic training
- Visiting MEPS to take the Oath of Enlistment and leave for basic training

In this part, we are going to break down the enlistment process into easy to follow sections. First we'll talk about the basic eligibility requirements for entering the Coast Guard. Next we'll discuss who recruiters are and what you can expect when you visit them. Then we'll cover the basics of the Armed Services Vocational Aptitude Battery test (the ASVAB). We'll move on to talk about Military Entrance Processing Stations and what happens in them. Finally we'll talk about the Delayed Entry Program and how to use it to get yourself in the best possible shape, both mentally and physically, before you leave for basic training.

9

Eligibility Requirements

Gone are the days when a recruiter could sign up an unwary young man in the morning and have him ship off to basic training in the afternoon. Today's military requires that its enlistees meet a lengthy list of requirements. In order to see if you meet those requirements, your recruiter and the personnel at the Military Entrance Processing Station (MEPS) you visit will look at your mental, physical, and moral qualifications. You will have to fill out an application, submit medical documentation, undergo a physical, and more. This is done so that the military is certain it is selecting the brightest and best young men and women to serve. Even minor physical or moral issues can become major problems on a battlefield and the military wants to catch them before that happens.

Before you even meet with a Coast Guard recruiter, you can get an idea of whether or not you might be qualified to enlist. The basic eligibility requirements are what a recruiter looks at when he or she meets you for the first time.

Basic Requirements

- Be between the ages of 17 and 27 (for active-duty enlistments)
  - 17-year-olds need their parents' permission to enlist
  - If you are enlisting as a reservist the upper age limit is 39
- Be a United States citizen or a legal permanent immigrant
  - There are some restrictions on immigrants from countries deemed hostile to the United States
  - Also non-citizens will not be eligible for jobs requiring security clearances

- Be a high school graduate
  - Only a very few GED holders are allowed into the Coast Guard each year
  - You must also have 15 or more college credit hours if you have a GED
- Score at least a 45 on the Armed Services Vocational Aptitude Battery (ASVAB) test
  - And your scores must qualify you for more than one 'A' school — the training schools you'll attend after you spend time working in at your first unit following basic training
- Have no more than two dependents (i.e. a spouse and/or one child)

If you do not meet these basic requirements, then you will more than likely not be able to continue with the Coast Guard enlistment process. Each branch's enlistment requirements are a little different, so if you do not qualify for one, you can always try to apply for one of the others. But the basic requirements are similar enough that you are better off trying to fix the issues that make you ineligible, such as your score on the Armed Services Vocational Aptitude Battery (ASVAB) test.

Alternatively, you can see if there is a waiver which would allow you to enlist despite not meeting some of the requirements. But waivers are a lot of work for recruiters and other military personnel, so they only want to do them for potential enlistees who are outstanding in other ways, such as those who speak a needed foreign language or who have extremely high ASVAB scores.

In addition to the basic eligibility requirements, there are some other factors to be considered. These can make you ineligible for Coast Guard service or might require a waiver in order to allow you to enlist (more on waivers in Chapter 12).

Other Eligibility Factors

- Tattoos: The Coast Guard has revised its tattoo and piercing policy as of 2009. Tattoos cannot extend below the wrist and should not be visible on the neck above the uniform collar. You may have a ring tattoo on your hand, but only on one finger per hand. Women may have tasteful, subtle permanent eyeliner. Tattoos cannot be racist, discriminatory, sexual, indecent, extremist, or gang related. Your tattoos and brands will be evaluated for content before you will be allowed to enlist.

- Body piercings: Females are allowed two holes in each earlobe to be filled with small, tasteful earrings. Body piercings that are visible outside of your uniform are not allowed and body piercings that are hidden by your uniform are strongly discouraged because of the likelihood of infection or damage during an active military career. Holes from former piercings should be healed and, if necessary, repaired.

- Dependents: The Coast Guard does not allow you to enlist as active duty if you have more than two dependents, including your spouse. (If you have more than two, but fewer than six, you might be able to enlist in the reserves.) Make sure that your spouse is able to care for your child without you for the eight weeks you will be gone and that he or she is willing to face the rigors of being part of a military family. If you have sole custody, you will need to have a Family Care Plan which spells out, legally, who will care for your child(ren) while you are in basic training and while you are deployed or if you are injured or killed.

- Drug and alcohol use: You are ineligible to enlist if you use illegal drugs and/or abuse alcohol. Your recruiter will ask about all previous drug use and you will be given a drug test as part of your enlistment physical and at basic training. Remember that one of the Coast Guard's primary duties is fighting the war against drugs, so extensive prior drug use is likely to make you ineligible. You should still answer truthfully about all drug use, even casual experimentation. Your recruiter will be able to tell you if your usage makes you ineligible or if a waiver will be required in order for you to enlist.

- Prescription drugs: You are ineligible to enlist if you are dependent upon prescription drugs, including insulin and ADHD medications (but excepting birth control pills used for birth control only, rather than to regulate your cycle). Your recruiter will have more information on which drugs may disqualify you for service and how long you will need to be off of them before being eligible for enlistment. But *do not* discontinue any legal use of prescription drugs without the consent of your primary physician.
- Medical history: Certain medical conditions will prevent you from enlisting. Because of the close quarters of Coast Guard boats and ships, you will not be allowed to enlist with some common allergies, such as peanuts, seafood, latex, bee stings, or wool. You will be required to reveal your medical history to the military and you will undergo a physical during your enlistment process. The doctors examining you will determine if any medical conditions are temporary (meaning you can enlist once your condition improves) or are disqualifying (meaning you cannot enlist or that you will need a waiver in order to do so).
- Criminal history: Some criminal convictions will render you ineligible for military service. You must disclose any prior criminal history (even sealed juvenile records) to your recruiter in order to apply to enlist. He or she will be able to tell you whether or not your criminal record makes you ineligible or if you will require a waiver to enlist. The Coast Guard is a law-enforcement branch, so they take your criminal history very seriously. Second and third degree misdemeanors and all felony convictions are disqualifying. Also the Coast Guard will do a background check and even look at your financial credit history.

All of these eligibility factors are considered when the Coast Guard is making the decision on whether or not you are eligible for enlistment. Some factors cannot be waived and will prevent you from enlisting, but these factors can vary between the branches. So if you are still interested in military service, but cannot enter the Coast Guard, you should speak with recruiters for the other branches and see if you might be eligible to serve with them.

Improving Your Chance for Eligibility

Before you begin the enlistment process there are some very simple steps you can take to make yourself a more eligible candidate.

- Finish school and further your education:
  - *If you are still in high school, stay there.* Do not drop out and do not waste your time. Study. Do your homework. Make decent grades (aim for at least a C+ average in all of your classes and you will do fine when you take the ASVAB). Try to take a mix of basic classes (math, science, English, history) and more technical ones or ones related to a field you might be interested in (computers, business, journalism, etc.).
  - *If you have finished high school, take classes at your local community college.* General education classes (math, science, English, history) will not only keep your mind fresh for the ASVAB, but getting them done now will save you time later if you decide to work towards your degree while serving in the military. Take your classes seriously, though, and strive to make decent grades.
  - *If you have dropped out of high school, you MUST get your GED before you can even consider enlisting.* Additionally, it is recommended that you have 15 credit hours of college classes under your belt. This will put you on the same consideration level as a high school graduate.
- Visit your family physician:
  - *You should get a full physical out of the way before beginning the enlistment process.* Not only will this alert you to any

79

problems which might hold up your enlistment, but your family doctor can advise you whether or not you can stop taking any drugs that have been prescribed for you. He or she can also tell you how to get in shape for enlistment.

- Exercise and eat right:
  - *According to a 2010 study at Cornell University, almost 12 percent of young men and over 30 percent of young women who are the right age for enlistment are ineligible due to not being able to meet weight standards.* Now is the time to lose weight, eat right, and exercise more. Your doctor is the best guide for this process. Never try to lose weight or begin an exercise program without consulting him or her first. Now is also a good time to stop smoking. It will improve your health and make you a stronger candidate.
- Avoid risky behavior:
  - *Do not drink (if you are underage) or drink excessively, use illegal drugs, break the law (including traffic violations), get tattoos or body piercings, bounce checks or get into financial trouble, have unprotected sex, etc.* All of these behaviors could lead to issues which will hinder your ability to enlist.
- Instead form healthy habits:
  - *Volunteer. Take up a hobby or a new sport. Get a part-time job. Take a class on a subject which interests you. Learn a new language. Stay current on the news.* All of these will keep your mind and body active and healthy, which will ultimately make you a better candidate for military enlistment.

Talking to Military Recruiters

Recruiters are active duty military personnel who are specially trained to select the young men and women who will join the branches of the service. They are your point of entry into the military, in general, and the Coast Guard, specifically. To put it simply, it is their job to decide if you are a good fit for the Coast Guard and if the Coast Guard is a good fit for you. Their advice can help you make the best decisions for your future. As has been mentioned before, you'll want to make sure that you meet with recruiters from all the branches of the service. A Coast Guard recruiter can only answer questions accurately about the Coast Guard and as each branch has something different to offer, it is in your best interest to meet with them all in order to get the most information on your options.

Meeting Your Recruiter

There are several ways in which you might meet a Coast Guard recruiter. If you take the Armed Services Vocational Aptitude Battery test (ASVAB) in high school, then your scores are usually shared with local recruiters. Assuming your scores are high enough to qualify for enlistment, recruiters will contact you, usually by phone. You may also give your information to the Coast Guard and request that a recruiter contact you. The easiest way to do this is to go to http://www.gocoast guard.com/ and click on "Get More Info." Calling your local Coast Guard recruiting station is a good option as well, though your "local" recruiter may be located in a different state! Because the Coast Guard is small, recruiters cover a wide area. They are not going to come to you; you will have to look for them. Also Coast Guard recruiters do not accept walk-ins. You will have to set up an appointment. This is because your recruiter may not always be in his or her office. Having an appointment guarantees that he or she will have time to see you without being interrupted by other commitments.

However you meet your recruiter, you want to be sure that you are comfortable with him or her. The recruiter is going to be your entry point into the Coast Guard and you need to be able to trust that he or she has your best interests in mind. The vast majority of recruiters are loyal, hardworking, honest, professional men and women who want to

U.S. Coast Guard recruiters will often go to community events as a way to meet potential enlistees (Official U.S. Coast Guard photograph by Damian R. Nastri).

make sure that they are adding the best of the best to the Coast Guard. They will tell you the truth and expect it from you in turn. Recruiters are trained in persuasion, much like salesmen, but they are also trained to act as your representative as you navigate the enlistment process. They do not work off of quotas, though they do have goals to meet each year. But those goals are often easily achieved — especially in the Coast Guard, which is a small branch with low turnover — and recruiters then have the luxury of being picky about the new enlistees they sign up.

However, there are a few recruiters who may not be completely aboveboard. If you ever feel uncomfortable about a recruiter for any reason, then you should stop working with them immediately. Look for another recruiter in the same branch of the service, but in a different office and explain — politely and calmly — why you have concerns about the first recruiter you spoke to. Your concerns will be taken seriously and looked into, especially if you are respectful about how you present them. If you are not comfortable speaking with another recruiter, because of anything that the first recruiter may have said or done, contact Coast Guard Recruiting (contact information is in the back of this book, under "For More Information").

Additionally, if you don't feel that you are completely "clicking" with your recruiter, speak to the other recruiters working in the same office. Personalities vary and you may find a better rapport with another recruiter.

Initial Meeting with a Recruiter

Once you have made contact with a Coast Guard recruiter, he or she will ask you to come in for an initial interview. This will give you a chance to learn more about what the Coast Guard has to offer you and for the recruiter to learn more about you, so that he or she can make sure you are qualified to enlist in the Coast Guard. That initial meeting with your recruiter is a job interview, so you should treat it as such and take it seriously. Here are some important tips:

- Before going into the meeting, do some basic research on the Coast Guard so that you will know more about its mission, history, careers, etc.
- Make an appointment and keep it. If an emergency comes up and you need to reschedule, call the recruiter immediately.
- Leave early enough so that you will not be late to the meeting. Don't forget to account for traffic and time to find a parking spot. Some recruiting offices can be tricky to locate, so you might want to get directions online or from the recruiter.
- Dress nicely — dress shirt, slacks, and possibly a tie for young men; a modest dress or a skirt or slacks with a blouse for young women.
- Turn off your cellphone or leave it in the car. Same for MP3 players.
- Shake hands, greet the recruiter by name and rank, and thank him or her for taking the time to meet with you.
- Be an active listener. Listen to everything the recruiter says and be sure to ask for clarification of any details you don't understand. Ask questions and listen carefully to the answers. Don't be afraid to ask "stupid" questions.
- Be open and honest. The military will do background checks on you, so you might as well tell the truth from the beginning.
- Be professional and respectful. You are interviewing the Coast Guard at the same time that the Coast Guard is interviewing you. Treat this as you would any job interview. If you've never interviewed before, look for some books on interviewing at the library or for interview tips online.

The recruiter will tell you if there is anything specific he or she needs you to bring with you, but you should always bring your:

- Driver's license
- Social Security card
- Birth certificate
- High school diploma

- College transcript (if applicable)
- Permanent resident alien (green) card (if applicable)

There are other items that are a good idea to bring with you. These will save both you and the recruiter time and will help you make sure you have all the information you need:

- A pen and a pad of paper for taking notes.
- Your parents or legal guardians.
  - ○ They will have questions too and many recruiters prefer that they be a part of the initial interview process. If you do not wish to include them or if you are not in contact with them, then you can bring a mature friend or a trusted adult. They are there to help you remember what is discussed. But know that the recruiter needs to ask personal questions about past drug use, medical issues, and more, so be sure that you are okay with talking openly in front of the person who accompanies you.
  - ○ Note: If you are 17, then your parents must come with you and their approval is required for you to be able to enlist.
- Your spouse.
  - ○ If you are married, your husband or wife should come with you. If you have children, though, they should stay with a baby-sitter so that you can have uninterrupted time to talk with the recruiter.
- Your résumé listing any jobs you've held since you were 16.
  - ○ Also bring the names of your supervisors and the addresses and phone numbers of your past and present jobs.
- Medical information.
  - ○ Bring what you know, but you will need to give the military a complete profile during the enlistment process, so the more information you can gather beforehand, the better.
- Information about any law violations, even minor ones like traffic tickets and even ones where your juvenile record was sealed.

- Names and phone numbers for several personal references, people who can speak to your character and personality.
  - These should not be family members. Make sure they have agreed to speak to any recruiters who call them.
- Goals you would like to accomplish in your life.
  - If the recruiter knows what you want to do, then he or she can help you see how the military might be able to help you meet those goals.

You should also bring any questions you have for the recruiter. These can be anything you want to know about the Coast Guard, the enlistment process, basic training, military service, etc. Think about these carefully and then type them out on a computer, so that you can easily read them. Again, don't be afraid to ask questions you think are dumb. The recruiter wants to answer all your questions and it's almost a guarantee that he or she has heard every question you could think to ask. Some possible questions:

- Can you explain the enlistment process to me from beginning to end?
- How does the Coast Guard differ from all other branches of the service?
  - You should know the basic answer to this from your research, but this will give the recruiter an opportunity to fill in any blanks.
- What do you like about being a Guardian? What do you dislike? Why did you become a Guardian?
- Can I speak with people whom you have recruited into the Coast Guard, both recently and in the past, so that I can find out more about their experiences in the Coast Guard?
  - Current service members are excellent sources of information. Remember to speak to them as politely and respectfully as you do the recruiter. Ask them about their experiences during the enlistment process, basic training, follow-on schooling, and in their first assignments. Ask them if they

are enjoying their work and if they plan on re-enlisting. Ask them what their impressions of your recruiter were.

- For potential enlistees who are female: Are there female Guardians I could speak with about their experiences?
    o They will be able to tell you what it is like to be a woman in the Coast Guard. Be sure to talk to both new female Guardians and ones who have served for some time. They will give you different perspectives.
- For potential enlistees who are homosexual or bisexual: Are there gay Guardians I could speak with about their experiences?
    o This request will probably be harder for your recruiter to fulfill, since gay service members have not been serving openly before 2011. Ask them about the experience of transitioning from serving under "Don't Ask, Don't Tell," about the experience of serving openly, and about any problems or issues they've face because of their sexual orientation.
- Can I visit a Coast Guard base or a reserve unit?
    o If you live near a base or a reserve unit this is a great way to see the Coast Guard in action before you enlist.
- What are the job possibilities available to me in the Coast Guard? What job did you do before you became a recruiter? Why did you pick that job? What did you enjoy about it? What didn't you like about it?
- How long are enlistment contracts for? How many years will I still obligated to the military after I finish my time in active duty?
    o Even after you finish your active duty commitment, you will still owe the military several years in the inactive reserves, where you can be called back up if needed.
- What rank will I be after basic training? Am I qualified to enter the service at an advanced rank?
    o This usually requires college credit, receiving Eagle Scout or the Girl Scout's Gold Award, several years' participation in JROTC, or a longer enlistment contract.

- How do promotions work in the Coast Guard? How often will I be promoted?
- Does the Coast Guard offer opportunities to move from enlisted to officer if I so choose?
- How do I choose my job in the Coast Guard? Can I select my job before basic training? How do Coast Guard jobs compare with civilian jobs? How will the skills I learn in the Coast Guard help me in civilian life?
- How will I be trained after basic training? What is job training like in the Coast Guard — mostly classroom settings or more hands on (or does it depend on the job)?
- How am I assigned to my first duty station? How often will I have to move?
- What is the likelihood I will be sent to war or deployed overseas?
  - This varies depending on the branch of the service. Even though the Coast Guard is charged with protecting the waters in and around the United States, Guardians can still be sent to fight in foreign wars, usually under the command of the Navy. Also, because Guardians are law enforcement officers and search-and-rescue personnel, they are more likely to find themselves in dangerous situations as a daily part of their job.
- How often will I travel as part of my job?
- What is basic pay? What supplemental pay and allowances are offered? What will I be required to cover from my paycheck (uniforms, etc.)?
- What education benefits does the Coast Guard offer? What strings are attached to any education benefits? How does the GI Bill work?
- What are benefits for spouses and families? What is life like on base? What type of housing will be assigned to my family?
- What enlistment bonuses are available? What are the requirements and the restrictions?
  - The Coast Guard does offer some enlistment bonuses or

extra money for signing up, but only your recruiter will have the information on what they are. *Do not* enlist simply for a bonus. They usually have strings attached that are more trouble than the bonus is worth.

- How do I make sure that what I sign up for (jobs, bonuses, benefits, rank, etc.) is what I actually get? What information is on my enlistment contract?
- What retirement plan is guaranteed for career Guardians? How many years do I need to put in? Will I still have health care when I retire?
- What is Coast Guard basic training like?
  - o This is covered in Part Four but your recruiter will have the most up-to-date information.
- Am I in good enough shape for basic training? If not, what would I need to do to improve?
- Can I contact my family during basic training?
- What happens if I get hurt or sick while I'm at basic training? What happens if I am unable to complete basic training for any reason?
- What programs do you offer during the Delayed Entry Program to help me prepare for basic training and military service?
- Can I come to any meetings and training sessions you have with new enlistees who are in the Delayed Entry Program?
  - o This will give you a chance to see how the Coast Guard helps new enlistees prepare. You will also be able to get a feel for the culture of the Coast Guard.
- Can I change my mind about joining the Coast Guard while I am in the Delayed Entry Program?
  - o As long as you have not taken the final Oath of Enlistment — which you take just before leaving for basic training — you are able to change your mind. Once you take the Oath, however, you are obligated to follow through on your contract.
- If I leave the Coast Guard after my initial enlistment period,

what services are available to help me transition back into civilian life? What happens to me if I have to leave before my enlistment contract is up?

These questions, asked during your initial meeting with your recruiter, will allow you to learn more about the Coast Guard, but the Coast Guard will also want to know more about you. You will fill out a non-binding application, which will give the recruiter the information he or she needs to see if you are tentatively qualified to enlist. You may also, at the recruiter's suggestion, take a mini version of the ASVAB in the recruiter's office. It will give you your basic score (which will tell you if you may be eligible for enlistment) and will let you know approximately how well you'll do on the full ASVAB test. (More on the ASVAB test in Chapter 13.) But you should *not* schedule any other testing at this time. The full ASVAB and your physical can wait until you are cer-

You should listen carefully during your meetings with a recruiter (Official U.S. Coast Guard photograph by PA3 Annie R. Berlin).

tain that you want to join the military and until you know which branch you want to enter.

The most important thing to remember about your initial meeting (and any follow-up meetings) is to listen actively. That means pay close attention to what the recruiter is saying and ask questions to further clarify. Do not let your mind wander. Do not get caught up in the excitement of dreaming of a star-spangled military career. There is time for that later. Now is when you need to be objective. Listen closely, ask questions for more information or to clarify, and take careful notes on what you hear. This is very important as you will need those notes later to compare the different military branches.

Second Meeting with a Recruiter

Take the information you learn during the initial meeting and think carefully about it for several days. Discuss the meeting with your parents or with the person who accompanied you. Consider whether the recruiter answered all of the questions you asked. Write down any new questions that occur to you. Compare what you've learned about the Coast Guard with what you learned during your meetings with the other branches of the service. This will help you see which branch will be the best fit for your goals and your personality.

The recruiter should, as you are leaving the initial meeting, schedule a follow-up meeting with you. If he or she does not, then request one. It should take place a few weeks after your initial meeting. The second meeting will be the time for you ask any final questions before you decide if you are going to choose the Coast Guard, if you are going to choose another branch of the service, or if you are going to choose not to enlist at this time or at all. The second meeting doesn't have to be as long. Take the time to ask any follow-up questions and then thank the recruiter for his or her time. Tell him or her that you will get back to them in a few days to let them know your decision. By this point, you should have met with recruiters from all branches so that you can make a fully informed decision.

Making Your Decision

If you decide that you would rather join a different branch, politely tell your recruiter that you have decided that branch will be a better fit for you. He or she might ask why you decided that the Coast Guard was not for you. You can tell them if you like, remembering to be respectful. He or she may also try to convince you to give the Coast Guard another look, but should ultimately wish you well. Do not allow any friendly (or non-friendly) feelings for a particular recruiter to change your mind. Your decision should be based solely on the research you have done and comparison between the branches to see which one best matches your goals and your personality.

If after your research, you ultimately decide that military service is not for you, thank your recruiter for taking the time to speak with you. Be polite, but firm, and tell him or her that you are not interested at this time. Tell him or her why you are putting off military service at this time. Your recruiter might have a suggestion for how you can serve anyway, if you so desire. For example, if you prefer to go to college full-time, then your recruiter might suggest you consider the reserves or apply for an ROTC scholarship. If you simply cannot or do not want to join at this time, but you think you might be interested at a later date, then you can tell him or her that you will get back in touch. However, if you think you will not ever want to join the military, say so. Recruiters want to hear the truth from you.

If you decide you do want to enlist in the military and the Coast Guard is the branch for you, then your recruiter will start the process of making sure you are fully qualified to enlist in the Coast Guard. You are not guaranteed entry into the Coast Guard or any other branch of the service. Your recruiter may agree that you are provisionally qualified for enlistment, but there are a number of physical, mental, and moral factors that have to be looked at before you can be completely cleared for enlistment.

The Qualification Process

After you decide that you definitely want to enlist in the Coast Guard, the next step is to fill out an enlistment application. This is a form which will follow you throughout the enlistment process all the way to basic training and will be the basis for getting approval to enlist and for your enlistment contract. That means everything on this form needs to be accurate, so read it slowly and carefully, asking questions about any sections you do not understand. Your recruiter will make sure that the information is filled out properly.

The most important thing to remember about the enlistment process is DO NOT LIE. Lying in order to enlist in the military is a felony and when — not if — the military discovers the lie, you will be prosecuted and discharged. You *must* answer all questions truthfully and you *must* provide information to the best of your ability. You will fill out forms to disclose every detail of your medical, legal, financial, and educational history. You must tell the truth about:

- Any past drug use (prescription or illegal)
- Any medical problems that were diagnosed and treated by a doctor (as opposed to ones you only suspect you might have, such as undiagnosed asthma or a "trick" knee)
- Any troubles with the law (even minor ones such as traffic violations and even ones where your juvenile record was sealed or expunged)
- Any pending legal actions (such as being a witness in a court trial or currently going through a divorce)
- Any financial issues (such as bankruptcy or bounced checks)

Not only should you never lie, but your recruiter should never ask you to lie or to omit information. If your recruiter asks you to change any information, if he or she tells you to leave something off of a form, or if he or she tells you to lie about any aspect of your history, then stop the enlistment process *immediately*. End all contact with that recruiter and report him or her to Coast Guard Recruiting. (That contact information is located in the "For More Information" section in the back of the book.)

Depending on your history, you might have some difficulty gathering all the required information. If you've lived and worked and gone to school in one town your whole life, you'll have an easier time finding the needed paperwork than if you've moved around your entire life. But your recruiter can help you hunt down missing information, and by talking to family members, school teachers and counselors, your doctor, and other professionals in your life you should be able to find every-

Enlisting in the Coast Guard is an important step in your life and should be carefully thought through (Official U.S. Coast Guard photograph by Petty Officer 1st Class NyxoLyno Cangemi).

thing. The more data you collect before you first meet with a recruiter, the less time will be spent searching for it after you make the decision to enlist.

Once you have filled out all of the required forms, your recruiter and other military personnel will go over them. They will be able to tell if you are qualified enough to continue in the enlistment process. There are some issues which will stop the process instantly. For example, if medical personnel at a local Military Entrance Processing Station (MEPS — the location where you go for your physical and to take the ASVAB) look at your medical questionnaire and determine that you have a serious medical issue which will not allow you to pass the required physical, then you will not be allowed to continue in the enlistment process. Unfortunately, there is almost no way to get around such a problem and you will not be allowed to join the military.

Some issues will render you ineligible, but might be able to be resolved with a waiver. Whether or not something can be waived is up to the main recruiting office, not your individual recruiter, though he or she can tell you if something definitely cannot be waived. Waivers take a lot of paperwork and you are more likely to get one if you have only minor issues needing to be waived, rather than if you have major problems. For example, if you smoked pot once three years ago and have never done any other drugs at any time, plus you have an application which otherwise qualifies you, then you are more likely to be approved for a waiver than if you have used drugs more regularly and have other problems which would delay the qualification process.

In addition to revealing any negatives from your past, you should also remember to detail any positives. The Coast Guard does allow you to enlist at a higher rank (E-3, rather than E-1) if you have done several successful years of military programs such as JROTC or ROTC or if you are an Eagle Scout in the Boy Scouts or have received the Girl Scout's Gold Award. (You can also enlist as an E-3 if you enlist with a six-year contract.) And volunteer work and other such initiatives show that you are a hard-working person who would be an excellent addition to the Coast Guard.

After your recruiter has made sure your enlistment application is completely filled out, that all of the information is accurate, and that you do not need any waivers in order to continue the enlistment process (or that you have received the waivers needed to continue), then you are ready to visit MEPS for your physical and to take the ASVAB.

Visiting the Military Entrance Processing Station (MEPS)

Military Entrance Processing Stations (MEPS) are Department of Defense facilities which exist to help evaluate and process potential military enlistees. They are located in almost every state, as well as Puerto Rico, and both civilians and members from every branch of the military work there. Thousands of applicants a year go through MEPS — getting physicals, taking the Armed Services Vocational Aptitude Battery (ASVAB) test, selecting military jobs, signing enlistment contracts, taking the Oath of Enlistment, and leaving for basic training.

Most enlistees will visit MEPS at least twice. The first time is for processing and evaluation of your physical and mental eligibility for enlistment. The second time is for final swearing in and departure for basic training. But everyone's circumstances vary and your MEPS experience will be shaped by any snags in your qualifications, by how far you live from a MEPS facility, by your type of enlistment (active duty or reserve), or by the branch in which you are enlisting. This chapter will give you the basic information on what to expect at MEPS so that you will be better prepared for your visit or visits.

Staying Overnight

Your recruiter will schedule your visit to MEPS after you have completed the initial qualification process discussed in Chapter 11.

Because he or she wants to be sure that you are on time and ready for your day or days at MEPS, generally you will be required to stay overnight the evening before at a hotel near your MEPS location. Your recruiter will make arrangements for your travel and lodging. Your food and hotel stay will be covered by the government, but it is important that you continue to behave professionally and maturely. At this time you are still being considered as an applicant for military service and any mistakes in judgment are likely to end your enlistment process immediately.

While you are at the hotel, you should:

- *Be respectful of your fellow applicants.* You will be sharing a room with at least one other applicant and you will not have a say in who your roommate is. Be polite and courteous and remember that much of military life is learning to work with those who are assigned to your team.
- *Be respectful of the other patrons of the hotel.* Do not make too much noise talking, watching TV, or playing music.
- *Be respectful of the military and the government.* They are covering the cost of your hotel room, but you will be liable for any additional charges. Do not make long distance calls or charge movies or internet service to the room. Remember to listen carefully to the instructions of the military liaison that is in charge of the applicants staying at the hotel. He or she is responsible for making sure that you know the rules and that you get to MEPS on time.
- *Get to sleep early.* Days at MEPS begin early and your wakeup call at the hotel will be as early as 4:30 A.M. Don't stay up too late or you will not be ready for the long day ahead of you. If you're worried that you won't be able to sleep in the unfamiliar environment, you might try sleeping with earplugs in. They can help block strange noises which might keep you awake.
- *Relax.* This is especially important if you are going to be taking the ASVAB the next day. Don't spend time cramming for the

test. It's more important that you rest up so that your brain is fresh for the test. (More on taking the ASVAB in Chapter 13.)

The military liaison will tell you the wakeup time. You will not have a lot of time to get ready (good practice for when you're in basic training!), so you might want to shower the night before. You should wear comfortable, neat clothing. You don't have to dress up, but you should look professional. A good suggestion is "business casual"—slacks and a nice shirt with closed toe shoes and socks. Do not wear hats, clothes with profane or obscene language and images, or jewelry/body piercings. (You'll just have to take any jewelry off for the medical examination anyway, so you might as well leave it at home where it will be safe.) You must wear underwear, including a bra for women.

Arriving at MEPS

After you are ready and you have eaten breakfast, you will be transported to MEPS for processing. It is important that you remember to bring everything with you that you will need, as you will not be able to return to the hotel to retrieve forgotten items.

Items to bring with you to MEPS include:

- Social Security card
- Birth certificate
- Driver's license
- Permanent resident alien (green) card, if applicable
- Eyeglasses and/or contacts and your prescription, if applicable
- Your medical history (your recruiter will help you get this together)
- Pen and paper, in case you wish to take notes on anything
- A book or magazine to read (you are NOT allowed to bring electronic devices, including cellphones, handheld games, MP3 players, etc.)
- Any other paperwork that your recruiter tells you to take

When you get to MEPS, you will pass through the metal detector and then you will begin the processing. Much of the visit to MEPS follows the old military adage of "hurry up and wait," so remember to be patient and to listen carefully to what MEPS personnel tell you to do.

The first visit to MEPS will usually include the following steps:

- Taking the ASVAB (unless you have already taken it within the past two years)
- Getting a complete physical, including blood work
- Talking to a representative from your branch about career opportunities
- Signing your enlistment contract
- Taking the Oath of Enlistment to enter the Delayed Entry Program (DEP); more on DEP in Chapter 14

It is important to pay attention to instructions while you are at the Military Entrance Processing Station (Official U.S. Army photograph by D. Myles Cullen).

If you have not yet taken the ASVAB, or if you need to retake it for some reason, then that will usually be the first thing you do at MEPS. Some enlistees will take the ASVAB on the afternoon of the first day and then return to MEPS the next day for the rest of their processing. Others will take the ASVAB first thing in the morning and then finish their processing that day. That leads to a very long, very stressful day, though, so it is best to avoid that if you can. Your recruiter will be able to tell you what your options are for taking the ASVAB during your MEPS visit. Chapter 13 tells all about the ASVAB test and the various ways in which it can be taken.

Medical Examination

Whether or not you have taken the ASVAB previously, you will definitely be getting your physical done while at MEPS. MEPS medical personnel will have already looked over your medical files, before you even arrive. The medical information you provided on your enlistment application was sent to MEPS for an initial pre-screening. This pre-screening allows MEPS personnel to rule out applicants who have obvious, major problems. It also gives them a chance to let your recruiter know if more information is needed about a medical issue from your past. That allows the recruiter to work with you to gather that information, so you can bring it with you when you visit MEPS. Then MEPS medical personnel will consider both that information and the information they gather via your medical exam to decide if you are qualified for enlistment, if you need a waiver in order to qualify, or if you are not qualified.

The doctors and nurses at MEPS are not tied to any particular branch of the military and they see potential enlistees from all five branches. Their job is to make sure that you are medically fit for military service. They are not trying to weed anyone out for personal reasons or because they are vindictive and they are not being overly picky about problems that may seem minor to you. They must consider the effect that a seemingly minor medical condition could have on a military unit during battle. They do not want to jeopardize the lives of military personnel by sending someone into battle who will not be able to hold up under fire. They also do not want to put you at risk by sending you for training with a medical issue which will lead you getting hurt or killed.

In order to get a full picture of your medical history and your current physical condition, the staff at MEPS give you a complete physical. This includes:

- Height and weight measurements — including a body-fat measurement if you exceed the weight requirements for your intended service
- Hearing and vision tests
- Range of movement tests — the doctors and nurses will make you stand in a line, wearing only your underwear (males and females are tested separately) and perform a series of movements designed to show problems with your bones, joints, ligaments, tendons, and muscles
- Blood work — for drugs and alcohol, HIV, pregnancy, and general health
- Urinalysis — for drugs and general health
- Medical interview — MEPS personnel will go over the information you provided on your enlistment application and ask you further questions about your medical history. As with the enlistment application, DO NOT LIE
- Specialized tests — if the doctors or nurses decide they are necessary in order to follow up on a suspected issue or problem

There are a lot of medical screenings done each day at MEPS, so during your visit you will spend a lot of time waiting. Remember to be patient and respectful. Bring a book or magazine to keep yourself occupied.

Talking with a Coast Guard Liaison

In addition to the Department of Defense personnel (doctors, nurses, testing staff, etc.) working at MEPS, there are also representatives from each branch of the service. The Coast Guard liaisons at MEPS are there to help you if you need them. While you should have your recruiter's phone number and other contact information with you just in case, the Coast Guard liaison will be the first point of contact for any issues you encounter during your visit. He or she can help clear up any problems, fill out paperwork, find needed documents, etc.

The liaison is also the person you will talk to after you complete your medical screening. He or she will go back over *everything* with you again — starting with your enlistment application, going through your medical, educational, and legal histories, and finishing up with any missing information. Though this repetition of information you already organized might seem annoying to you, it is the military's way of making sure that only the best personnel are enlisted. Your talk with the liaison is the chance to make sure that all parts of your application are accurate, so, one more time, DO NOT LIE. Make sure all information is correct and, if not, make sure the corrections are made. The liaison will be making sure you are fingerprinted and that a background check is done, so any discrepancies will be discovered.

For some branches of the service, the time spent with the military liaison is the time in which you will select your job, but not in the Coast Guard. The Coast Guard will offer you a class on available Military Occupational Specialties (MOSs) while you are in basic training, but you will not select your job until you have graduated and gone to your first duty assignment. (More on basic training and life after basic training in Part Four.) For now, you will simply make sure that all the needed information is part of your packet, so that when the time comes to select your MOS your details will be available.

Oath of Enlistment

After you have successfully completed the ASVAB, the medical tests, and the meeting with your Coast Guard liaison and all personnel have determined that there are no further issues which will prevent you

Taking the Oath of Enlistment is the last part of your visit to the Military Entrance Processing Station (DoD).

from enlisting in the Coast Guard, then you are ready to take the Oath of Enlistment. This will be the first of two Oaths you take. This Oath of Enlistment installs you into the Delayed Entry Program in an inactive reserve status. The second Oath will be taken the day you leave for basic training and it will install you into the active-duty military. (If you are enlisting into the reserves, then you will only take the Oath once. As soon as you take it, you are a member of the military and the reserves.)

The Oath of Enlistment is a serious, solemn occasion. You should not take it lightly. If, after going through processing at MEPS and talking with your recruiter and Coast Guard liaison, you have any doubts at all about enlisting, then do not take the Oath. It is better to temporarily disappoint your recruiter than to sign up for something you do not want. Read over the Oath carefully and make sure you are able to agree to it, freely and clearly.

> *I, _____, do solemnly swear (or affirm) that I will support and defend the Constitution of the United States against all enemies, foreign and domestic; that I will bear true faith and allegiance to the same; and that I will obey the orders of the President of the United States and the orders of the officers appointed over me, according to regulations and the Uniform Code of Military Justice. So help me God.*

The Oath is administered at MEPS by military officers. Your family is welcome to attend and to take photographs afterward. If for some reason they cannot attend, MEPS or your recruiter can often stage the Oath at a later time so that they can take pictures then.

After the Oath

After you have sworn the Oath, you will return to the Coast Guard liaison to verify your paperwork. He or she will congratulate you on your decision to enlist in the Coast Guard and will instruct you on proper behavior during your time in the Delayed Entry Program. Make sure you get his or her contact information, so that you can get in touch with them if needed. Then you can head home.

Your recruiter will receive your paperwork and should call you within a day or two of your return from MEPS. If he or she doesn't call, you should call and schedule a time to go over your paperwork again. Any problems or errors *must* be corrected before you leave for basic training, so it is crucial that you proofread your documents as many times as you can. You will also need to schedule a time to meet with your recruiter to talk about what you can do to prepare for basic training during your time in the Delayed Entry Program. Chapter 15 has some basic tips for how to get ready.

Taking the Armed Services Vocational Aptitude Battery

One of the basic requirements of enlistment is the Armed Services Vocational Aptitude Battery test or the ASVAB. The ASVAB gives the military an idea of what your skills are and what jobs you might be suited for. In this section we'll look at what the ASVAB is, how it is administered, what tests make up the ASVAB, what the scores mean, and how you can work on improving your scores.

What Is the ASVAB?

The ASVAB is basically a test of your knowledge and skills. The military wants to know what you already know about math, science, language, electronics, mechanics, and more, and it wants to know what skills — or aptitude — you have for jobs in various fields. By knowing what you are or might be good at, the military can place you in a job where you can succeed. This is good for both you and the military. If you're successful in your job, then you're more likely to be happy and a happy enlistee is one who is more likely to stay in the military.

To test your knowledge and skills, you take the nine tests that are part of the ASVAB. These tests make up the two parts of the ASVAB: the Armed Forces Qualifying Test (or AFQT) and the technical subtests. Nine tests may sound like a lot, but the individual tests are not long and you do not have to master every one of them. The technical subtests are designed to show the military what skills you have, so that they can match you with a job. The AFQT, however, is the part of the test that will determine whether or not you even qualify to enlist in the military, so it is important that you at least do well on those tests.

How Do You Take the ASVAB?

There are several ways you can take the ASVAB. Many high schools will administer the ASVAB to their students. The students can then use their scores to discuss their aptitudes with their guidance counselor. Since the ASVAB is designed to tell you what you are good at or what you may be good at, it is useful as part of a career decision-making process. If you take the ASVAB at your school, your personal information may be shared with recruiters. They can then contact you to tell you more about the opportunities available to you in the military. If you met your recruiter this way, then he or she can use the scores from the ASVAB you took at school to determine both your eligibility to enter the military and the jobs available to you. ASVAB scores are good for two years, so even if you take the ASVAB in high school, but don't decide to enlist until a year after graduation, your scores are still valid.

However, if you did not take the ASVAB in high school, you will have to take it as part of the enlistment process. At the beginning of your time talking to a recruiter, he or she may give you a mini–ASVAB test (called a Computer Adaptive Screening Test [CAST] or an Enlistment Screening Test [EST]) right in the recruiting office. This test will give both you and your recruiter an idea of how you will probably score on the AFQT portion of the ASVAB. If you do well on that mini-test, then you will likely do well on the full ASVAB. (See the section to come on ASVAB scores for more information on how the test is scored and what your scores mean.)

When you go to take the full ASVAB, you will take it at either a Military Entrance Processing Station (MEPS) or a Mobile Examining

Team (MET) site. MEPS is a facility that is run by the Department of Defense (DOD) to assist and streamline military enlistment for all branches of the service. (See Chapter 12 for more information on MEPS.) MET sites exist solely for the purpose of administering the ASVAB. There are two ways of taking the ASVAB: Computer Adaptive Test (CAT) and Paper and Pencil (PAP). Most MEPS facilities only give the CAT and most MET sites only give the PEP. You are tested on the same type of information, regardless of which type of test you take, but the method of testing is fairly different. Though it is more likely you will take the CAT, you should know how to take both types, because you could end up taking the PAP.

Computer Adaptive Test (CAT)

The CAT is taken on a computer. You will use a mouse to select your answers, though you will have scratch paper provided for working

The Computer Adaptive Test is one way you may take the ASVAB (DoD).

out your answers. But the CAT is not just a computer version of the pencil and paper test. Instead it adapts as you answer questions. The first question for each test will be of medium difficulty. If you get it right, then the second question is a little harder, but if you get the first question wrong, then the next one is easier. You cannot, however, choose the order in which you answer questions in order to answer the easier ones first. You have to take the questions as they are given to you.

The entire CAT takes however long it takes you to finish, though each section has a time limit. Answers are input and then finalized. Once they are finalized, you cannot go back and change them. You keep answering questions until time is up or until you finish the section. Once you finish one section, you move immediately into the next. You cannot go back and check answers on sections you have already finished. You will receive your scores at the end of the test.

PAPER AND PENCIL TEST (PAP)

This is a traditional standardized test, using test booklets and bubble sheets you fill in with pencils. The questions vary in difficulty throughout the test. Within a section, you can answer questions in any order you like, which allows you to quickly answer the easier questions and then go back to the harder ones.

Once a section starts you answer questions until you finish or until time is up. If you finish early, you can go back and check your answers and change them if you need to, but you cannot go on to the next section. The PAP test takes about three to four hours. Your scores are mailed to your recruiter within a few days from when you take the test.

How Many Questions Are on the ASVAB?

The number of questions on the ASVAB depends upon whether you take the CAT or the PAP.

#	Name of Test Questions	Type*	CAT # of Questions	CAT Time	PAP # of Questions	PAP Time
1	General Science	Tech	16	8 mins	25	11 mins
2	Arithmetic Reasoning	AFQT	16	39 mins	30	36 mins
3	Word Knowledge	AFQT	16	8 mins	35	11 mins
4	Paragraph Comprehension	AFQT	11	22 mins	15	13 mins
5	Mathematics Knowledge	AFQT	16	20 mins	25	24 mins
6	Electronics Information	Tech	16	8 mins	20	9 mins
7†	Auto Information	Tech	11	7 mins	25	11 mins
	Shop Information		11	6 mins		
8	Mechanical Comprehension	Tech	16	20 mins	25	19 mins
9	Assembling Objects	Tech	16	16 mins	25	15 mins
		Total:	145	154 mins	225	149 mins

*Tech = Technical.
†Auto and Shop Information is two separate tests on the CAT and one combined test on the PAP.

What Tests Make Up the ASVAB?

ARMED FORCES QUALIFYING TEST (AFQT)

- Arithmetic Reasoning (AR): Basic word problems based on mathematical situations you might encounter every day. Designed to test your ability to reason and solve problems.
- Mathematics Knowledge (MK): General math problems at a high school level, including algebra and geometry. Designed to test your knowledge of mathematics.
- Paragraph Comprehension (PC): You will read paragraphs and answer questions based on what you read. Designed to test your ability to analyze written material.

- Word Knowledge (WK): Questions about the meanings and use of words. Designed to test your vocabulary and communication skills.

TECHNICAL TESTS

- Assembling Objects (AO): You are shown drawings of objects and must answer questions about how they fit together. Designed to test your ability to use spatial reasoning.
- Automotive and Shop Information (AS): Quizzes you on automobile mechanics, tools, shop terminology, uses of parts, etc. Designed to see what you know about mechanics and mechanical work.
- Electronics Information (EI): Questions about circuits, electrical systems, electronics terminology, radio principles, etc. Designed to see what you know about electronics and working with electrical and radio components.
- General Science (GS): Basic science questions — life, physical, earth — at a high school level. Designed to test your knowledge of science.
- Mechanical Comprehension (MC): Tests you on mechanical and physical science principles. Designed to see what you know about how machines work, how mechanics affect real life, etc.

What Do the ASVAB Scores Mean?

There is no overall score on the ASVAB. Instead, there are two separate groups of scores which are important: your AFQT percentile and your composite scores.

THE AFQT PERCENTILE

The AFQT percentile is what determines your eligibility to enlist. It is derived by this formula: 2(VE) + AR + MK. That means that your scores from Paragraph Comprehension (PC) and Word Knowledge

(WK) are combined to create a Verbal Expression score. That score is then added to your Arithmetic Reasoning (AR) and Mathematics Knowledge (MK) scores to give your AFQT raw score. The raw score is compared to the scores of ASVAB test takers who participated in a study in 1997. That comparison allows the test to determine your AFQT percentile. So, if your AFQT percentile is 53, that means that your raw score was better than 53 percent of the test takers in that study.

The military divides the AFQT scores into categories, which are then used to determine a potential enlistee's eligibility. When the military's recruitment goals are lowered (meaning they don't need as many personnel) or when there are more people applying for enlistment than needed, then they usually raise the acceptable AFQT scores for potential enlistees to make sure they are only bringing in the best recruits.

Category	*AFQT Percentiles*	*Category*	*AFQT Percentiles*
Category I	100–93	Category IVA	30–21*
Category II	92–65	Category IVB	20–16*
Category IIIA	64–50	Category IVC	15–10*
Category IIIB	49–31	Category V	9–0†

*Any potential enlistees in Category IV must have a high school diploma, not a GED. Also, only 20 percent of enlistees in the entire military can be from Category IV.

†You are not eligible to enlist in the military if you are in Category V.

Each branch of the military has a different minimum AFQT score. As of September 2010, those were:

Branch	*Minimum AFQT w/HS Diploma*	*Minimum AFQT w/GED*	*Notes about GED Holders*
Air Force	36	65	The Air Force allows less than 1 percent of its yearly enlistees to have GEDs. GED holders who have 15 or more college credits are considered the same as those with high school diplomas.

Branch	Minimum AFQT w/HS Diploma	Minimum AFQT w/GED	Notes about GED Holders
Army	31	50	The Army only allows 15 percent of its yearly enlistees to hold a GED. GED holders who have 15 or more college credits are considered the same as those with high school diplomas.
Coast Guard	45 — and your scores must qualify you for A Schools (training after basic	45 — and your scores must qualify you for A Schools (training after basic)	The Coast Guard has very tight limits on the number of GED holders it accepts. Anyone wanting to enlist in the Coast Guard with a GED must also have completed 15 or more college credits.
Marine Corps	31	50	The Marine Corps allows less than 5 percent of its yearly enlistees to have GEDs. GED holders who have 15 or more college credits are considered the same as those with high school diplomas.
Navy	35	50	Very few GED holders are allowed into the Navy and those that are must not have any issues requiring a waiver. GED holders who have 15 or more college credits are considered the same as those with high school diplomas.

COMPOSITE SCORES

Your composite scores are what determine which jobs you are eligible for. Each branch of the military has a different way of calculating those scores and determining which scores go with which military job. For the current information on how each branch calculates its composite scores and which scores go with which job, visit *http://us military.about.com/od/joiningthemilitary/a/asvabjob.htm* or check out the latest edition of Rod Power's *ASVAB for Dummies* (Wiley Publishing), which has information on which subtests correspond to which military job.

Retaking the ASVAB

If you do not score well enough on the AFQT portion of the ASVAB to qualify for enlistment, you can retake the ASVAB, but not right away. You have to wait thirty days to retake the ASVAB a second time and then wait six months to retake it a third time. Your most recent score is the one which is used to determine your eligibility. Each branch of the military, though, has limits on whether or not you can retake the ASVAB simply to increase your scores in order to qualify for a particular job or enlistment bonus or for a reason other than having an AFQT percentile that is too low for enlistment. Your recruiter can give you the most up-to-date information on his or her branch's restrictions.

The best thing you can do to improve your scores is to brush up on your basic math, science, and vocabulary skills. A high AFQT will open up opportunities for you in the military. You'll be more likely to qualify for waivers (if needed), to qualify for enlistment bonuses, and to qualify for other incentives. Also, because your ASVAB scores remain valid while you are a member of the military, you can use them later on to qualify for advanced training or reclassification into a different job field, though they are not used to determine promotions or awards.

Studying for the ASVAB

Your first step should be go purchase an ASVAB study guide. You can also check them out from the public library or your school or college library, but there may be long waiting lists and you will not be able to write in the library's copy. If you prefer to practice online, check to see if your public library or school or college library has access to an online test prep program. They might and, if so, it will be free to use. Or, to work on your math, science, and language skills, you can use March 2 Success, a free online test preparation program sponsored by the United States Army. You can sign up here: *https://www.march2success.com.* (Using the site does not obligate you to enlist in the Army and they do not share your information with Army recruiters.) March 2 Success does not have a specific ASVAB practice test, but it offers programs to help you boost your basic skills.

Take the sample tests in the study guide or online. They will show you what areas you need improvement in. Then focus your study to those areas. The ASVAB is testing science, math, and vocabulary on a high school level, so if you have been out of school for a time or if you have a subject you were not as good at, then you'll definitely need to brush up your skills.

Though the study guide or online program will have a lot of questions and several sample tests, you should not assume that the questions on the sample tests are the same as those that will be on the actual ASVAB. The ASVAB questions are closely guarded and no study guides — either in print or online — will have access to them. Instead the study guide questions are meant to give you an idea of what type of questions will be on the actual ASVAB and what areas you need to improve in.

Study Tips

- *Be sure to study in a quiet place with good lighting and a firm sur-face for writing.* Music is okay, if it's not so loud that it distracts you, though you're probably better off sticking with instrumental music, rather than songs with lyrics.

- *Make sure you have all the supplies you need before you begin studying.* Pencils and scratch paper are vital, but you should not have a calculator around to tempt you as you will not be able to use one on the test.
- *Include a stopwatch or a clock so that you can time yourself.* When you take practice tests, you'll want to be sure that you mimic testing conditions, including time limits.
- *Study in longer blocks.* You'll want to set aside an hour or two for each study session. That will allow you the time to focus and absorb information.
- *While occasional study groups can be helpful, make sure you mostly study by yourself.* You won't have anyone to rely on when you take the test, so you need to be sure you can do it on your own.
- *Take notes during your study sessions.* Taking clear notes will help you remember information. Besides, you'll have to take notes in your classes during basic training, so you might as well practice that skill now!
- *Set goals for what you want to accomplish and when.* Your main goal is to do as well as you can on the ASVAB, but also have smaller goals that will help you focus and give you a feeling of accomplishment. Small goals are a good way of breaking your studying into more manageable chunks. You could set a small goal for how much you want to cover in a particular study session or week.
- *Continue practicing even when you aren't studying.* The best way to improve your math and verbal scores is to use your skills all day, every day.
  - o *Read the newspaper and a wide variety of books.* Even reading books that are light and fun will help you improve your vocabulary. As you are reading, jot down words you don't know and then look them up in a dictionary. Write down the definition and then make sure to use that word in conversation some time that same day.

    o *Use mental math whenever possible.* Rather than reaching for a calculator, do the problem in your head while you're shopping, out to eat, paying bills, etc. Doing quick math problems in your mind or on paper will keep your math skills sharp.

Preparing for the Test

- *Get plenty of sleep the night before.* Don't stay up studying. Last minute cramming will not put the information into your brain and it might interfere with the information you already know.
- *Eat a light breakfast with some protein (eggs, bacon, etc.).* That will help you keep from getting hungry during the test. Have a glass of water to drink, but don't overdo it. You don't want to have to go to the bathroom in the middle of the test.
- *Assemble your supplies the night before.* Your photo ID, pencils and scratch paper are the most important. Bring your glasses, even if you wear contacts. Wear a watch (with a second hand if possible) to help keep track of time.
- *Get to the testing site early.* You'll want to be there at least fifteen minutes before the test starts, so that you can handle any administrative tasks and not feel rushed. Be sure to account for traffic. You might even consider doing a test drive over to the testing facility a day or two before.
- *Reschedule if needed.* If you wake up and feel sick or if you are injured or if you have recently had a stressful event happen, then you won't be at your best to take the test. You can always reschedule. Just call your recruiter and he or she will handle it.

Taking the ASVAB

Your recruiter will arrange the time and location for you to take the ASVAB. He or she will help you work out any transportation issues, such as if you need to stay overnight the evening before the test. If you are taking the ASVAB at MEPS, you may be doing it at the same time as your physical, which can make for a long day or couple of days. But whenever and wherever you take the ASVAB, there are some basic strategies which can help you do better on the test.

DURING THE TEST

- *Relax.* It is just a test. If you are calm, then you will automatically do better on it.
- *Listen to or read all instructions carefully.* If you don't understand, ask the person administering the test to explain.
- *Work steadily, but don't rush.* Getting questions correct is more important than the number of questions you get through. You'll want to answer as many questions as possible, but not at the expense of getting questions wrong.
- *Make sure to read every question carefully.* Be sure that you understand what information is being asked for. Then read all of the answer choices provided to you.
- *Think carefully about what you think the answer is.* Then think about it again.
- *Eliminate logically.* Look at the answer choices. In a multiple choice test, two of them are usually obviously wrong. That leaves two that are possibilities. Choose the one that you think is the best possible answer.
- *If your answer does not match any of the answer choices, then look back over the question.* See if you need to think about things in a different way or look at the answer in a different direction.
- *When in doubt, guess.* As long as you have eliminated some of the answer choices logically, then if you really do not know, make a guess about one of the two remaining choices. You are not penalized for wrong answers; you just don't get a point for them.

Your recruiter is always the best person to ask about the ASVAB. He or she knows the most up-to-date information about the ASVAB and can walk you through the process of studying for it, taking it, and understanding your scores. When you've done the best you can do on the ASVAB, the scores will not only assist you in the enlistment process, but will also reveal more about your career skills. Taking the ASVAB will teach you more about who you are and what careers you might enjoy.

14

Joining the Delayed Entry Program

Unlike in the past, when you might have gone to MEPS, done your testing and physical, signed your papers, and left for basic training the next day, nowadays almost every person who joins the military enters the Delayed Entry Program (DEP) first. It is extremely rare to leave for basic training any sooner than two weeks after visiting MEPS and most enlistees spend six weeks or more in DEP before departing for training. The military uses the DEP because it allows them to better manage their numbers, spreading out new recruits evenly throughout the year. The branches of the military have set numbers of personnel they have to maintain each year and they need to carefully plan how many personnel are added each week, month, quarter, etc.

The amount of time you spend in the DEP depends on many factors. Recruiting staff and training staff start by looking at the current enrollment in basic training and figuring when those people will be finished. They also have to look at when people who are currently in DEP will be able to leave for training and figure when they will be done. Then they have to factor in the eight weeks you'll be spending in training and they get an idea of when you can leave for basic. That date can be up to 365 days from the time you took the Oath of Enlistment to enter the DEP. Generally new Coast Guard enlistees have a long wait because of the small training facility and low turnover (not many people leave the Coast Guard each year). And that's good news, because the time you spend in DEP is time you have to prepare for basic training. By getting yourself ready — physically, mentally, educationally, financially — you will set yourself up for success in basic training. The more preparation you have, the better you will do during training.

Behavior in the DEP

Unless you are enlisting in the reserves, you will not be paid during your time in the DEP. (Reserve enlistees can begin attending training sessions with their unit even before attending basic and be paid for their time.) Instead you are a member of the inactive reserves until you ship off to basic. Even though you are not being paid, you still have work to do and expectations you must live up to. Your recruiter and the Coast Guard liaison at MEPS will brief you on those expectations, but it doesn't hurt to go over them here as well.

- *Behave like a Guardian.* Your time as in DEP should not be spent partying and slacking off. You are expected to uphold the values of the Coast Guard and to carry yourself as a Guardian.
- *Prepare yourself for recruit training.* Because Coast Guard recruiters cover a wide area (most are responsible for enlistees from parts of several states), you will not have regularly scheduled meetings with your recruiter. He or she expects you to work on your own to prepare for basic training. In the next chapter we will go over all the ways you can set yourself up for success during basic training.
- *Finish school.* If you are still in high school when you enlist, you MUST graduate and you must do so on time. Otherwise you will jeopardize your enlistment.
- *Keep in touch with your recruiter.* Alert him or her to any changes in your situation, from major ones like marriage or legal problems, to minor changes such as changing addresses.

Leaving the DEP

Because you are not a full member of the Coast Guard during your time in the DEP, you can change your mind about enlisting and leave the DEP with no serious repercussions. HOWEVER, this is a very serious step and should only be taken in extreme situations. You should not go through the stages of the enlistment process — talking to a recruiter, visiting MEPS, taking the Oath of Enlistment — without sober consideration of the decision you are making. By the time you enter the DEP, you should be certain of your choice and eager to prepare for basic training.

But things can happen during your time in the DEP which might cause you to have to change your mind about enlisting. A scholarship to college, the death of a family member, pregnancy, trouble with the law, a serious injury — these are all situations which could arise and prevent you from completing your obligation. The first thing you should do is speak with your recruiter and you should do that as soon as you realize there is a problem. Schedule a time to speak privately and inform him or her of your situation calmly and rationally.

You should know that your recruiter will try very hard to keep you from leaving the Coast Guard. By this point in the process the Coast Guard has spent a lot of time and money getting you approved to enlist. They feel that you will be an asset to the Coast Guard and they aren't going to want to lose you. Your recruiter will try to come up with other options to help you out, such as changing your ship date, getting you approved for a college Recruit Officer Training Corps (ROTC) program, etc. But if your reasons are valid and solid and there is no way you can enlist because of your situation, then they will have to approve your request. You may have to write a letter to the Coast Guard Recruiting outlining your reasons for leaving the DEP. The address is in the "For More Information" section in the back of this book.

If your situation is temporary — an injury or a family emergency, for example — and you still want to enlist in the Coast Guard at a later date, then you will likely be able to, though you might need a waiver to do so. Tell your recruiter if you think that might be the case, so that he or she can help you out. But if you are just experiencing "buyer's remorse" and you want to leave the DEP because you no longer want to be a Guardian, then you will more than likely not be considered to be a good candidate for enlistment if you change your mind again in the future. So think carefully before making any decision.

Using the DEP to Prepare for Recruit Training

The best thing you can do during your time in the DEP is to prepare to leave for basic training. You can get yourself in the best possible shape, which will make your time in recruit training easier. The next section has information on how you can prepare mentally and physically.

Preparing for Basic Training

All enlistees worry about basic training. They wonder if they'll be able to keep up physically; they stress about being away from friends and family; they aren't sure how they'll cope with being ordered about all day. Unfortunately the only way to know how you're going to do in basic training is to go through it. Everyone's basic training experience is different, so there is no way to prepare for all the fears, stresses, and hardships you'll face. But the Delayed Entry Program gives you the time to prepare to face *most* of those fears, stresses, and hardships. If you work hard before you leave for basic, then you'll be ready to work hard during basic, which is what will make you a successful recruit.

There are four ways you should prepare yourself for basic training: physically, mentally, socially, and emotionally. Each of these is as important as the others. By working on them all, you'll insure that you have the best possible start to your basic training experience.

Physical Preparation

Because the physical fitness portion of basic training is what worries enlistees the most and because poor physical fitness sets you up for failure during basic training, physical training is the first aspect of preparation you should focus on. If you are in good physical condition when you leave for basic training, you will find yourself with one less worry during your time there. Your recruiter will give you guidelines for how to get yourself in shape for basic training and he or she may even exercise with you, but ultimately you are responsible for your own physical conditioning.

STARTING AN EXERCISE ROUTINE

The first thing you should do before beginning any exercise routine is to consult with your family physician. MEPS should have caught any serious medical problems, but your doctor should still check you out to make sure you are physically ready for an exercise program. A check-up will also help to catch any physical problems which could delay you when you get to basic training. You don't want to get all the way to training and then discover that you aren't in good enough shape to start!

If you can afford to, joining a gym or a YMCA is a good idea. The staff there can help you plan an exercise program which meets your needs, fits your body, and will get you ready in the time you have. But if you cannot afford a gym, you can still prepare on your own. Your recruiter may have a training guide, which will walk you through the process of getting in shape. You can also check your public, school, or college library for books on exercise and look for exercise plans on the internet. If you are still in high school, talk to your gym teacher or ROTC instructor about helping you plan a workout program. Or, if you are no longer in high school, check with a local college to see if they offer a degree in physical education. If so, talk to one of the professors and see if they would consider giving a student extra credit if they plan a training regimen for you.

Important things to remember as you set up an exercise program:

- *Vary your exercises.* Only focusing on running will not help you develop a healthy level of physical fitness. Be sure that you include all three of these activities:
  - Flexibility exercises (which prevent injury): warm-up and cool-down stretches
  - Cardiorespiratory workouts (which increase your heart rate and improve breathing): running (outdoors is best; don't just

A mile and a half run is part of the physical fitness assessment in basic training (Official U.S. Coast Guard photograph by Petty Officer 2nd Class Christopher D. McLaughlin).

run on a treadmill), swimming, biking, rollerblading, active sports
  o Muscular strength activities (which help build muscle): sit-ups/crunches, push-ups, pull-ups (or flexed arm hangs for women), working out on exercise machines or with weights
- *Start slowly.* If you fling yourself immediately into a hard training regimen, you will get injured. Injuries, either during the DEP or during basic, will delay your training which could affect your job training placement, thereby affecting your ability to get the job you want. A severe enough injury could even prevent you from becoming a Guardian.
- *Be consistent.* Work out three to five times a week for 45 minutes to an hour at a time. Try to work out at the same time each day so that your body gets used to the routine.
- *Be patient.* If you cannot run a mile when you start training, that's okay. That is why you are training. Start by walking, then add in jogging, gradually increasing the amount of jog-

ging and decreasing the amount of walking. Before you know it, you'll be running!

- *Gradually progress.* Add a little on to your workout each week, not so much as to overload your body, but enough to make sure you are consistently challenged.
- *Aim for endurance, not speed.* Though you will have some timed runs during basic training, most of the runs and hikes you will do will focus on endurance. During your preparations you should start out with longer, slower runs. This will allow you to build up the lung and muscle strength to go the distance when needed. As you train, you will find that you are able to add more miles into the same amount of time.
- *Watch your form.* You'll want to learn the correct, Coast Guard way of doing sit-ups and push-ups, so that you do not waste your practice. Your recruiter can help you practice.
  - o *Push-ups*: Start with your hands under your shoulders, arms straight, feet together behind you, toes curled under. Lower down until your arms are past a 90 degree angle. Your body should stay in one line while you do a push-up.
  - o *Sit-ups*: Lie on your back with your feet flat on the floor, knees bent. Put your hands behind your head and do not interlace your fingers. Raise your upper body until your elbows touch your knees and then lower your body back down until your shoulder blades touch the floor again. You may not lift your rear end off of the floor. A friend can hold your feet for you, if needed.
- *Set a goal.* Halfway through Coast Guard basic training, you will take a physical fitness assessment. The assessment tells the Coast Guard if you are in shape enough to handle the rigors of being a Guardian. If you don't pass the assessment, then you will be made to work out for an extra hour each morning, time you'd rather spend sleeping. If you don't pass the assessment when you take it a second time, then you will not graduate Coast Guard basic training.

But, if you train towards the assessment while you in the DEP, then you'll be more likely to pass it. You will be working during your first four weeks of basic training to try to get in the best shape possible, but it is still a good idea to aim close to the assessment standards before you even get to basic training. That way you will ensure that you are in the best shape possible at the beginning of basic training and that you are able to easily pass the assessment.

Here are the physical fitness assessment requirements and what you should aim for:

Event	*Assessment Minimum — Men*	*Assessment Training Goal — Men*
Run	1.5 mile run in 12 min. 51 sec.	1.5 mile run in 13 to 14 min.
Push-ups (in 60 sec.)	29	25
Sit-ups (in 60 sec.)	38	35

Event	*Assessment Minimum — Women*	*Assessment Training Goal — Women*
Run	1.5 mile run in 15 min. 26 sec.	1.5 mile run in 15 to 16 min.
Push-ups (in 60 sec.)	23	20
Sit-ups (in 60 sec.)	32	30

- *Stay alert to prevent injury.* Pay attention to what your body tells you. Muscle soreness is normal when starting an exercise routine, but if it seems extreme or if you injure yourself, visit your doctor immediately. Minor problems can become major ones if left untreated.
- *Dress the part.* Proper workout attire will help prevent injuries.
  - Wear clothes that are appropriate to the weather. Avoid plastic suits designed to make you sweat, even if you need to lose weight. These will cause you to overheat and get sick.
  - Wear shoes that work for your feet. Good running shoes don't have to be expensive, but they do need to be properly

fitted. Go to a store that specializes in running shoes and get the associates there to assist you in finding the right shoes.

- *Work out with a friend.* You are more likely to maintain and succeed in an exercise program if you have someone to support you. Working out with a fellow enlistee, your recruiter, a friend, or a parent is a great way to get in shape and enjoy yourself at the same time.

- *Have fun.* Exercise can be fun if you allow yourself to enjoy it. In addition to working on the running, sit-ups, and push-ups you'll need to be prepared for at basic training, treat yourself to a fun exercise once a week. Join a team sport, take a dance or aerobics class, go for a hike or a bike ride, etc. These treats can keep you interested and engaged in your exercise program.

OTHER PHYSICAL PREPARATION

Besides working out, you'll also want to prepare your body in other ways. By leaving for basic training with the healthiest body possible, you'll be less likely to get sick while you're there.

- *Eat right.* If you haven't already been eating a healthy diet, now is the time to start. Your physician can help you learn more about which foods you should be eating and which you should cut back on. You can also visit the Department of Agriculture's healthy eating website *http://www.choosemyplate.gov* for more information.

  There are a few easy changes you can make which will help your transition to the dining facilities at basic training.
  o *Cut out fast food and sodas and cut back on desserts.* You won't have access to them (or only very limited access), so you might as well get used to doing without now.
  o *Learn to eat quickly and quietly.* Try to eat two of your meals a day in just 10–15 minutes each without talking to anyone, which is about what you'll be doing at basic training.

o *Drink water.* Water is better than anything else you can drink, including milk, juice, or sports drinks. Try to drink at least eight 8-ounce glasses a day.

o *Eat a balanced meal.* Make sure you include plenty of fruits and vegetables and that you aren't just eating meat and starches (like bread or potatoes).

- *Lose weight sensibly.* The Coast Guard has weight standards you must meet. Your recruiter will tell you if you are above those standards. But be sure to lose weight slowly and carefully. No matter how much you need to lose overall, you should never lose more than 1 to 2 pounds per week. Do not go on a crash diet to lose weight, because you will only rebound later and gain the weight back. Instead learn to eat low fat, healthy meals and be sure to exercise (especially aerobic exercise) regularly.

- *Stop smoking and drinking.* You will not be able to smoke or drink while you are in basic training. Quitting now will not only help you during training, it will also improve your health and make sure you are in good shape before you leave. (It should go without saying that you aren't doing illegal drugs and that you aren't drinking or smoking if you are underage.)

- *Change your sleeping habits.* While in basic you will get up very early every day, often as early as 4 or 4:30 A.M., though sometimes earlier than that. Now is the time to learn how. Start going to bed around 9 or 10 P.M. and getting up between 4:30 and 5 A.M.

If you live in a location that is in a different time zone from Cape May, New Jersey (which is where Coast Guard basic training takes place), it is a good idea to start adjusting to that time zone about one or two weeks before you leave. For example, Cape May is on Eastern Time. If you live in Wyoming (which is on Mountain time), then you are going to want to go to bed between 7 and 8 P.M. (Mountain time) and get up between 2:30 and 3 A.M. (Mountain time).

- *Toughen your feet.* Start walking in boots now and you will be better prepared for walking in them at basic training. You can use hiking boots if you have them or get a pair of military boots from a military surplus store. Just make sure that your boots fit properly and that you do not run in them. (Almost all running in basic training is done in athletic shoes.)
- *Practice proper hygiene.* Basic training means living in close quarters with other people and that means you'll be more likely to get sick, even though the personnel at basic training do their very best to prevent illnesses. If you make it a habit to wash your hands often, especially before eating and after coughing, sneezing or going to the restroom, then you will decrease your chance of illness.
- *Learn to swim.* All Guardians have to pass a swim test. Your instructors will teach you if needed, but learning before you go will save you valuable time during basic. You don't want to wait until you're partway through basic to find out that you are unable to overcome a fear of water. (If you are already terrified of the water and refuse to learn to swim, then the Marine Corps, the Navy, and the Coast Guard are NOT the right services for you.)
- *Practice safe sex.* If you get pregnant during your time in the DEP, you will not be allowed to go to basic training. If your wife or girlfriend gets pregnant, then it can also cause complications for you. The Coast Guard will not let you leave basic training to attend the birth, and more than likely won't let you leave your first duty post either. You will also have to work out how you are going to help support your child while you are still only a junior enlisted Guardian. Additionally, all recruits are tested for sexually transmitted diseases when they arrive at basic. Being diagnosed with one will more than likely get you sent back home.
- *Avoid injuries, body modifications, drug use, etc.* Drive carefully. Don't take silly physical risks. Do not get a new tattoo or body piercing. Do not use illegal drugs and check with your

recruiter to be sure that any new prescription drugs will not disqualify you.

Mental/Educational Preparation

FINISHING SCHOOL

If you are still in high school when you enlist in the Coast Guard, then the most important thing you can do during the DEP is to finish school. If you do not graduate, then you will not be allowed to leave for basic training. You don't have to make straight As, but you should work hard, study carefully, ask your teachers for help if you need it, and stay out of trouble. If it looks like you might not graduate or if another school related problem, such as a suspension, arises, alert your recruiter immediately.

KEEPING YOUR BRAIN SHARP

A smart Guardian is a good Guardian. Just as you work out to keep your body healthy, you want to work your mind to keep it healthy. Basic training isn't just about physical education. There is a lot of learning that will take place during your eight weeks and you want to get your mind ready to soak it all in. Here are some tips for brain workouts:

- *Practice taking notes.* There will be classes in classrooms and in practical settings during basic training and you will be tested on what you learn. You'll want to be able to take effective notes even when you are tired. The public library will have books on note taking or you can check out the resources at *http://www.collegeboard.com/student/plan/college-success/955.html.*
- *Turn off the TV and reduce computer and videogame time.* You will not have access to a television, computer, or videogames while you are at basic training. Start getting used to that now by

making them an occasional treat, rather than an everyday habit. Use the extra time to work out, visit with friends and family, read, or learn military skills in advance.

- *Work on math skills.* If you do not feel that your mathematics skills are where you want them to be, now is the time to work on them. No matter what your job in the Coast Guard, you will use math. The public library will have books on math to help you brush up. One easy way to improve is to stop using a calculator and do all math problems in your head or by hand on paper.
- *Read.* The Coast Guard has an official reading list, which can be found at *http://www.uscg.mil/leadership/resources/readinglist.asp.*

  The list includes four sections, each with books on a specific topic. The sections are:
  - *Leader of Leaders Section*: books that have been recommended by Senior Coast Guard leaders
  - *Contemporary Issues Section*: books about challenges and changes being faced in America and around the world today
  - *Leadership Section*: books that focus on the skills needed to become an outstanding leader
  - *Coast Guard History and Culture Section*: books specifically about the Coast Guard, its past and its future

  Each year, if he so desires, the Commandant of the Coast Guard picks one title to be the "Commandant's Choice." There was not a selection in 2011, but the 2010 selection was *Rescue Warriors: The U.S. Coast Guard, America's Forgotten Heroes* by David Helvarg. The Commandant did not make a choice in 2009 or 2008, but the picks from other previous years were:
  - 2007 — *The Contrarian's Guide to Leadership* by Steven Sample
  - 2006 — *Alexander Hamilton* by Ron Chernow
  - 2005 — *Built to Last: Successful Habits of Visionary Companies* by Jim Collins and Jerry Porras

○ 2003 — *Character in Action: The U.S. Coast Guard on Leadership* by Donald Phillips and ADM James Loy, USCG (Ret.)
○ 2002 — *The Founding Fathers on Leadership: Classic Teamwork in Changing Times* by Donald Phillips

THINGS TO LEARN IN ADVANCE

You will learn a lot during recruit training; that is what your eight weeks there are for — learning. But there are things you can go ahead and start learning before you even leave for recruit training. Learning these things in advance will save you the trouble of having to learn them while you are tired, sore, and stressed. Some of the things you can learn are specific to the Coast Guard and will help you understand more about its culture and values. Other items are general to all branches of the military and will be used by you on a daily basis while you are serving in the Marines. All of these things will be taught to you again while you are at recruit training, but learning them now will save you some brainpower in the future.

Information Specific to the Coast Guard

Coast Guard's Birthday. The Coast Guard's birthday is August 4, 1790.

Coast Guard Chain of Command. The chain of command tells you who reports to whom. The chain starts at the top with the President of the United States and works its way down to the person directly in charge of you. (The members of the Department of Homeland Security are always civilians.) You will be expected to know the chain of command as it applies to you — title, rank (if applicable), and name of each person — but you will not know the names of some personnel until you get to basic training. Below is the Coast Guard chain of command listed in order.

• Commander-in-Chief (aka, The President of the United States)
• Secretary of Homeland Security
• Coast Guard Commandant

- Commanding Officer (CO)
- Executive Officer (XO)
- Training Officer (TO)
- Regimental Officer (RO)
- Battalion Officer (BO)
- Battalion Commander (BC)
- Section Commander (SC)
- Lead Company Commander (LCC)
- Company Commander (CC)
- Recruit

Coast Guard Core Values. Each branch of the military has its own core values. These are the qualities that they feel are most important for their members to focus on. During recruit training these values are studied extensively and during a service member's career they are expected to live up to these qualities.

The Coast Guard's core values are "Honor, Respect, and Devotion to Duty."

- *Honor* means always acting at the highest moral and ethical standards and remembering that the public must trust the Coast Guard for it to succeed in its missions.
- *Respect* means treating everyone with fairness, dignity, and compassion, working as a team, and valuing everyone's differences.
- *Devotion to Duty* means serving the United States with pride and hard work.

Coast Guard Ensign and Seal/Emblem. An ensign is a sea-going word meaning "flag." The Coast Guard's ensign was established in 1799 in a letter written by Secretary of Treasury Oliver Wolcott. The red and white stripes are meant to represent the thirteen original colonies of the United States. The only change to the ensign since 1799 is the addition of the Coast Guard's seal, a pair of crossed anchors.

Coast Guard History. One of the aspects of Coast Guard basic training is learning about the Guardians in whose footsteps you will follow. You will find out who they were, where they served, and what their

The Coast Guard Ensign (U.S. Coast Guard).

accomplishments were. This is important so that you understand how the Coast Guard has evolved into the force it is today. Since you will be tested on this knowledge while you are in basic training, you should read up on the history of the Coast Guard before you leave for recruit training. Chapter 6 has a basic overview of the history of the Coast Guard and you can find suggestions for books and websites in the "For More Information" section in the back of the book.

The Coast Guard Anthem and Hymn. The Coast Guard Anthem is

The Coast Guard Seal/Emblem (U.S. Coast Guard).

Semper Paratus (Always Ready). Captain Francis Saltus Van Boskerck wrote the words and music in 1927, though the words have been altered several times over the years. The final version was approved in 1969. You can download audio clips of the music at *http://www.uscg.mil/top/downloads/anthem.asp*.

> *From Aztec shore to Arctic Zone*
> *To Europe and Far East,*
> *The flag is carried by our ships*
> *In times of war and peace;*
> *And never have we struck it yet*
> *In spite of foeman's might*
> *Who cheered our crews, and cheered again*
> *For showing how to fight.*
>
> *CHORUS: We're always ready for the call,*
> *We place our trust in Thee.*
> *Through surf and storm and howling gale*
> *High shall our purpose be,*
> *"Semper Paratus" is our guide,*
> *Our fame our glory, too,*
> *To fight, to save, or fight and die!*
> *Aye! Coast Guard, we are for you.*
>
> *SURVEYOR and NARCISSUS,*
> *The EAGLE and DISPATCH,*
> *The HUDSON and the TAMPA,*
> *The names are hard to match;*
> *From Barrow's shore to Paraguay,*
> *Great Lakes or ocean's wave,*
> *The Coast Guard fought through storms and winds,*
> *To punish or to save.*
>
> *CHORUS*
>
> *Aye, we've been "Always Ready"*
> *To do, to fight, or die*
> *Write glory to the shield we wear*
> *In letters in the sky.*
> *To sink the foe or save the maimed*

Our mission and our pride,
We'll carry on 'till kingdom come
Ideals for which we've died.

CHORUS

The Coast Guard Hymn is "Eternal Father, Lord of Hosts," written in 1955 by Chief Warrant Officer George H. Jenks, Jr. It is the tenth stanza of the hymn "Eternal Father, Strong to Save," which is the hymn of the United States Navy. The tune can be heard here *http://www.cyber hymnal.org/htm/e/t/eternalf.htm*:

Eternal Father, Lord of hosts,
Watch o'er all those who guard our coasts.
Protect them from the raging seas
And give them light and life and peace.
Grant them from Thy great throne above
The shield and shelter of Thy love.

Coast Guard Motto. The Coast Guard's motto is *Semper Paratus.* This means "Always Ready."

Coast Guard Organization. The Coast Guard divides the United States into nine districts (plus one world district) which used to be numbered, but now have geographical names. (The numbers had become non-sequential because of reorganization over the years.) The unit map can be found here: *http://www.uscg.mil/hq/capemay/active-duty/Map3.asp.*

- Atlantic Area districts:
  - *Northeast Atlantic* (former District 1) — Headquartered in Boston, MA; Covers Maine, Vermont, New Hampshire, Massachusetts, Rhode Island, Connecticut, New Jersey, and half of New York
  - *Mid-Atlantic Area* (former District 5) — Headquartered in Portsmouth, VA; Covers most of Pennsylvania, Maryland, Delaware, Virginia, and North Carolina
  - *Southern Atlantic Area* (former District 7) — Headquartered

in Miami, FL; Covers South Carolina, most of Georgia and most of Florida

  o *Gulf Coast and Western Rivers* (former District 8)—Headquartered in New Orleans, LA; Covers half of Minnesota, part of Pennsylvania, Georgia, and Florida, most of Illinois, Indiana, and Ohio, and all of Kentucky, West Virginia, Alabama, Mississippi, Louisiana, Texas, Tennessee, Arkansas, Oklahoma, Missouri, Iowa, Kansas, North Dakota, South Dakota, Nebraska, Wyoming, Colorado, and New Mexico

  o *Great Lakes Area* (former District 9)—Headquartered in Cleveland, OH; Covers half of New York and Minnesota, part of Pennsylvania, Ohio, Indiana, and Illinois, and all of Michigan and Wisconsin

- Pacific Area districts:

  o *Pacific Coast* (former District 11)—Headquartered in Alameda, CA; Covers California, Nevada, Utah, and Arizona

  o *Pacific North West* (former District 13)—Headquartered in Seattle, WA; Covers Montana, Idaho, Washington, and Oregon

  o *Hawaii & Guam* (former District 14)—Headquartered in Honolulu, HI; Covers Hawaii and Guam

  o *Alaska* (District 17)—Headquartered in Juneau, AK; Covers Alaska

- PATFORSWA Area—Patrol Forces Southwest Asia; these are the Coast Guard patrol boats who are assisting the Navy in operations around the Middle East

Coast Guard Rank Structure. Rank structure is what tells you the level a military member has reached in the organization. You will be able to tell someone's rank by the markings on their uniform.

Before you leave for training, you should at least learn the rank insignia for the Coast Guard, though it is a good idea to go ahead and learn about the rank structures for all branches of the military. During your time in the Coast Guard, you will interact with personnel from all five branches, but you are especially likely to work with those in the Navy, so if you know Navy insignia as well, then you're ahead of the game.

The enlisted and officer ranks for all five branches of the military are shown on pages 140 and 141.

Creed of the Coast Guardsman. The Creed of the United States Coast Guardsman was written by Vice Admiral Harry G. Hamlet.

> *I am proud to be a United States Coast Guardsman.*
> *I revere that long line of expert seamen, who by their devotion to duty and sacrifice of self, have made it possible for me to be a member of a service honored and respected, in peace and in war, throughout the world.*
> *I never, by word or deed, will bring reproach upon the fair name of my service, nor permit others to do so unchallenged.*
> *I will cheerfully and willingly obey all lawful orders.*
> *I will always be on time to relieve, and shall endeavor to do more, rather than less, than my share.*
> *I will always be at my station, alert and attending to my duties.*
> *I shall, so far as I am able, bring to my seniors solutions, not problems.*
> *I shall live joyously, but always with due regard for the rights and privileges of others.*
> *I shall endeavor to be a model citizen in the community in which I live.*
> *I shall sell life dearly to an enemy of my country, but give it freely to rescue those in peril.*
> *With God's help, I shall endeavor to be one of His noblest Works....*
> *A UNITED STATES COAST GUARDSMAN.*

Coast Guard Guardian Ethos. The Coast Guard adopted the Guardian Ethos in 2008 as a way to tie all of the Coast Guard's various missions into one easy-to-understand identity. The Ethos defines the essence, the core, of what the Coast Guard is. Currently, as of 2011, the Ethos is being revised, but the 2008 version is as follows:

> *I am America's Maritime Guardian.*
> *I serve the citizens of the United States.*
> *I will protect them.*
> *I will defend them.*

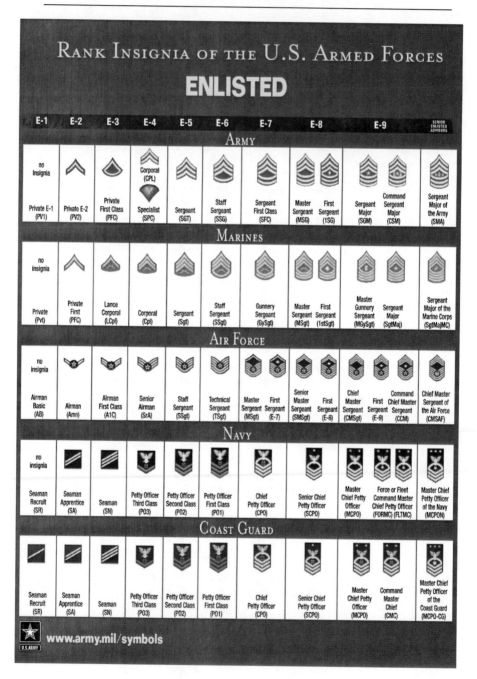

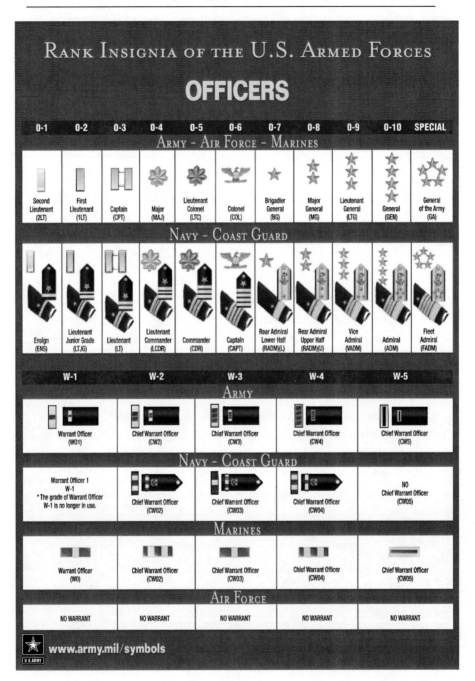

RANK INSIGNIA OF THE U.S. ARMED FORCES

OFFICERS

| 0-1 | 0-2 | 0-3 | 0-4 | 0-5 | 0-6 | 0-7 | 0-8 | 0-9 | 0-10 | SPECIAL |

ARMY - AIR FORCE - MARINES

| Second Lieutenant (2LT) | First Lieutenant (1LT) | Captain (CPT) | Major (MAJ) | Lieutenant Colonel (LTC) | Colonel (COL) | Brigadier General (BG) | Major General (MG) | Lieutenant General (LTG) | General (GEN) | General of the Army (GA) |

NAVY - COAST GUARD

| Ensign (ENS) | Lieutenant Junior Grade (LTJG) | Lieutenant (LT) | Lieutenant Commander (LCDR) | Commander (CDR) | Captain (CAPT) | Rear Admiral Lower Half (RADM)(L) | Rear Admiral Upper Half (RADM)(U) | Vice Admiral (VADM) | Admiral (ADM) | Fleet Admiral (FADM) |

| W-1 | W-2 | W-3 | W-4 | W-5 |

ARMY

| Warrant Officer (WO1) | Chief Warrant Officer (CW2) | Chief Warrant Officer (CW3) | Chief Warrant Officer (CW4) | Chief Warrant Officer (CW5) |

NAVY - COAST GUARD

| Warrant Officer 1 W-1 * The grade of Warrant Officer W-1 is no longer in use. | Chief Warrant Officer (CWO2) | Chief Warrant Officer (CWO3) | Chief Warrant Officer (CWO4) | NO Chief Warrant Officer (CWO5) |

MARINES

| Warrant Officer (WO) | Chief Warrant Officer (CWO2) | Chief Warrant Officer (CWO3) | Chief Warrant Officer (CWO4) | Chief Warrant Officer (CWO5) |

AIR FORCE

| NO WARRANT | NO WARRANT | NO WARRANT | NO WARRANT | NO WARRANT |

www.army.mil/symbols

I will save them.
I am their Shield.
For them I am Semper Paratus.
I live the Coast Guard Core Values.
I am a Guardian.
We are the United States Coast Guard.

Information General to All Branches of the Military

General Orders of a Sentry. The general orders are what you do when you are standing guard. You will be expected to know — by heart — the general orders. The Coast Guard, Marine Corps, and Navy have eleven general orders, while the Army and Air Force have a condensed, three-item list of orders. Here is the Marine Corps version:

1. *To take charge of this post and all government property in view.*
   - You are in charge and no one can change your orders except for the instructor who gave them to you.
2. *To walk my post in a military manner, keeping always on alert and observing everything that takes place within sight or hearing.*
   - You must always be on guard and aware of what is going on around you.
3. *To report all violations of orders I am instructed to enforce.*
   - This means that you must tell your instructor about any and all problems that occur while you are on guard, such as if someone tries to enter without authorization.
4. *To repeat all calls from posts more distant to the guardhouse than my own.*
   - You have to pass along information, even if phones or radios go out.
5. *To quit my post only when properly relieved.*
   - You cannot go off duty until the next guard assumes his or her post.
6. *To receive, obey, and pass on to the sentry who relieves me, all orders from the Commanding Officer, Field Officer of the day, Officer of the Day, and all Officers and Petty Officers of the Watch.*

- You have to tell the guard who relieves you about any special orders that you were given to follow.

7. *To talk to no one except in the line of duty.*
   - Guard duty is not a time for relaxing or hanging out.
8. *To give the alarm in case of fire or disorder.*
   - Again, you must stay alert for any problems.
9. *To call the Petty Officer of the Watch in any case not covered by instructions.*
   - This means you should ask if you encounter a situation that you do not know how to handle.
10. *To salute all officers and all colors and standards not cased.*
    - "Colors and standards" means the American flag. "Cased" means when it is not flying.
11. *To be especially watchful at night and during the time for challenging, to challenge all persons on or near my post, and to allow no one to pass without proper authority.*
    - This means you must make every person who approaches your post halt and clearly identify themselves and you can only let them pass if they have permission per the instructions you have been given.

Military Alphabet. The branches of the military have a shared phonetic alphabet. A phonetic alphabet is an alphabet where a sound or a word represents a letter. You know how when people spell something over the phone and the letters "b" and "v" or "t" and "p" sound very similar? That's why the military uses the phonetic alphabet instead. "Bravo" and "Victor" sound very different and keep personnel from getting letters confused when communicating. Here is the military phonetic alphabet:

Letter	Phonetic Word	Letter	Phonetic Word
A	Alpha	N	November
B	Bravo	O	Oscar
C	Charlie	P	Papa
D	Delta	Q	Quebec
E	Echo	R	Romeo
F	Foxtrot	S	Sierra

Letter	Phonetic Word	Letter	Phonetic Word
G	Golf	T	Tango
H	Hotel	U	Uniform
I	India	V	Victor
J	Juliet	W	Whiskey
K	Kilo	X	X-Ray
L	Lima (LEE-ma)	Y	Yankee
M	Mike	Z	Zulu

Military Time. Military time is designed to prevent confusion when information is communicated between personnel, just like the military alphabet. Military time is based on twenty-four hours rather than twelve. You do not have to use A.M. or P.M., because all of the hours are different. The word "zero" is used in every spot that doesn't have a number 1–9 and you do not use a colon between the hours and the minutes. So 2:05 A.M. would be Zero two zero five or 0205.

Time	Military Time	Pronunciation
12 A.M.	0000	Zero-zero-zero-zero
1 A.M.	0100	Zero one hundred
2 A.M.	0200	Zero two hundred
3 A.M.	0300	Zero three hundred
4 A.M.	0400	Zero four hundred
5 A.M.	0500	Zero five hundred
6 A.M.	0600	Zero six hundred
7 A.M.	0700	Zero seven hundred
8 A.M.	0800	Zero eight hundred
9 A.M.	0900	Zero nine hundred
10 A.M.	1000	Ten hundred
11 A.M.	1100	Eleven hundred
12 P.M.	1200	Twelve hundred
1 P.M.	1300	Thirteen hundred
2 P.M.	1400	Fourteen hundred
3 P.M.	1500	Fifteen hundred
4 P.M.	1600	Sixteen hundred
5 P.M.	1700	Seventeen hundred
6 P.M.	1800	Eighteen hundred
7 P.M.	1900	Nineteen hundred

Time	Military Time	Pronunciation
8 P.M.	2000	Twenty hundred
9 P.M.	2100	Twenty-one hundred
10 P.M.	2200	Twenty-two hundred
11 P.M.	2300	Twenty-three hundred

Military Terminology. As you can see, the military likes to use its own words and abbreviations. This can be confusing until you get used to it. Your recruit company commanders will be more than happy to tell you what they want you to call things, but if you get a basic grasp of terms before you leave for training, you'll feel less like you wandered into foreign country. There is a glossary in the back that has basic terms used throughout this book and there are several sources of information online:

- The Department of Defense: *http://www.dtic.mil/doctrine/dod_dictionary*
- TodaysMilitary.com: *http://www.todaysmilitary.com/inside/military-glossary*
- Naval Terminology [from the Navy's Bluejacket Manual]: *http://bluejacket.com/sea-service_tradition.htm*
- The Helmsman [has terms as well as a host of other things to learn before basic training]: *http://www.uscg.mil/hq/capemay/docs/pdf%20docs/Helmsmannew.pdf*

Uniform Code of Military Justice. The Uniform Code of Military Justice (UCMJ) is the body of military law. Parts of it spell out what happens to military personnel when they break the law. While you do not need to memorize the UCMJ (it's too long for that), you should read it over. As soon as you take the final Oath of Enlistment and leave for basic training, you are bound by the UCMJ and can be court-martialed for infractions. The parts of the UCMJ can be found here: *http://www.law.cornell.edu/uscode/html/uscode10/usc_sup_01_10_10_A_20_II_30_47.html.*

Your Social Security Number. The Coast Guard will need you to fill out many forms, right when you first arrive at basic training, while you're still shell-shocked. Your Social Security number will need to be written on almost all of them, so it is important that you have it memorized before you arrive. It is also a good idea to know just the last four digits of your number as that is often used to identify you while you are in the military.

WHAT YOU DON'T NEED TO LEARN IN ADVANCE

One aspect of preparing for recruit training might surprise you — you do not need to learn how to handle a weapon before you leave for training. Qualifying with a weapon is not a requirement in Coast Guard basic training, though if your job later on in the Coast Guard requires you to handle a weapon, then you will have to qualify at that time. The Coast Guard does teach you the basics of handling a weapon and they have a specific way they teach recruits to shoot. They've found that those recruits who enter basic training never having handled a weapon are much more likely to successfully complete the handgun course than those recruits who have grown up around guns. That's because recruits who have never fired a weapon don't have to unlearn poor habits, whereas the recruits who are more familiar with firearms don't always listen as carefully to instructions and then make mistakes.

The best way you can prepare for military weapons training is to relax and not worry about it. Your instructors will teach you everything you need to know and as long as you don't stress about it, you will do just fine. If you already know your way around a gun, then your best bet is to forget everything you have learned and go into Coast Guard training willing to start learning about weapons from the basics on up. Be open to learning the Coast Guard way to shoot and be eager to listen to everything your instructors tell you and you will qualify quickly.

You also do not have to learn how to drill, or march in formation, before you leave. Your instructors do not expect you to know how to drill when you arrive and they will begin showing you the basics as soon as you arrive.

Social Preparation

In addition to preparing your mind and body for the basic training experience, you will need to make sure to put your bills and other affairs in order. That way problems will not arise while you are in training and unable to deal with them. Also, you will need to get your friends and family ready for you to be gone.

GETTING YOUR AFFAIRS IN ORDER

There are things you will need to be sure to organize before you leave because you will not be able to take care of them while you are in basic training.

- *Open a bank or credit union account.* If you do not already have an account with a bank or a credit union, you will need to open one. Your recruiter can tell you what credit unions are common to Coast Guard bases, if you prefer to have an account at one of them. Otherwise, you can simply choose a bank that is convenient to you at this time. Be sure to get a debit card and to verify that it works before leaving for basic training.
- *Set up direct deposit.* Your recruiter will have the form for you to set up direct deposit of your military pay into your bank or credit union account. NOTE: Military pay can take 30 to 45 days to get started in direct deposit, so it is a good idea to have some money in your account in case of emergencies. One to two hundred dollars will work if you can afford it.
- *Bills.* You will not have access to your bank account, a computer, a check card, etc. while you are in training. Here are some suggestions for handling bills for your house, car, etc.:
    o *Pay off as many as possible.* If you leave for basic training debt free, then you won't have bills hanging over your head after graduation.
    o *Arrange for automatic payments.* Any bills that you cannot

147

pay off should be set up to be automatically paid from your bank or credit union account.

o *Have a trustworthy person handle them.* If you are married, this will be your spouse. Otherwise, choose someone who is financially responsible. A drinking buddy or someone you are dating is not a good choice.

- *Car.* If your car or other vehicle is paid off, does not have great sentimental value to you, and is not needed by your family, then you might consider selling it so that you don't have to worry about it while you're gone. Otherwise, arrange for the payment to be made automatically. If you leave it with someone, make sure they are trustworthy and that either your or their insurance will allow them to drive it if that is okay with you. Or you can arrange for it to be kept in storage until after graduation. If your driver's license or vehicle registration will expire while you are gone, see if you can go ahead and renew them before you leave.

- *Cellphone.* Check with your cellphone company to arrange for a military hold on your account. That way you won't have to pay for minutes you aren't using during basic training.

- *Paperwork.* Make sure you have copies of the documents you may need at basic training. These could include your marriage license, divorce paperwork, Social Security card, etc. While you're gone, important papers should be stored in a fireproof safe and the key should be given to a trustworthy family member or friend. If you are married, make sure that you give your spouse power of attorney which will allow them to sign in your name while you are away. Your recruiter can help you get the correct form and fill it out.

- *Legal issues.* You will not be able to leave for basic training with outstanding legal issues. Resolve any legal problems as quickly as possible and avoid getting involved in any new issues, even minor ones such as traffic violations. Keep your recruiter apprised of any legal problems you encounter during the DEP.

GETTING YOUR FAMILY AND
FRIENDS READY FOR YOUR ABSENCE

Leaving family and friends for eight weeks is hard for you, but it will also be hard on them. You can help ease their pain before you leave and they can help support you while you're gone.

- *Encourage them to write to you.* During Coast Guard recruit training you will not be able to receive or make phone calls that often, so mail is very important way for you to stay in contact with your friends and family. You can get mail every day except Sundays and holidays. You will be given time to write home, so ask your friends and family to write to you.

  Letters from home should be upbeat and cheerful. Ask them to help you keep your spirits up by offering words of encouragement. Bad news is sometimes unavoidable, but it helps if family and friends use their letters to you to relay mostly good things that happen. Even simple details of home life can help. They are welcome to send pictures, but care packages are not allowed.

  To help ensure you receive letters, partially address and stamp envelopes to yourself before you leave. You'll find out the rest of the needed information for your address once you get to training and you'll have the opportunity to send it to your friends and family so that they can write to you. Your address will be:

  > SR [Seaman Recruit] _____
  > Recruit Company _____
  > Healy Hall, or James Hall, or Munro Hall
  > USCG Training Center
  > 1 Munro Avenue
  > Cape May, NJ 08204–5083

- *Help your children understand what you'll be doing.* If you are a parent, then you'll need to prepare your kids for your absence.

There are books for younger readers about the Coast Guard in the "For More Information" section. Reading these with your child will help him or her understand your new job. You can also watch some of the videos about recruit training listed in that section, so that they can see what you'll be experiencing. Ask your kids to write to you every day and promise that you'll write to them as well.

- *Have a going away party.* This is a great way to enjoy time with friends and family, but there are a few things to keep in mind.
  - *Don't have the party the night before you leave.* You'll want to be rested, not tired from staying up all night. Instead have your get-together the weekend before you leave.
  - *Don't use drugs at the party, do not have unprotected sex, and do not drink if you are underage.* Drugs and alcohol in your system will be discovered upon your arrival at basic training and unprotected sex could lead to pregnancy or a disease. All of these will keep you from completing training.
- *Remind them that you love them and that their support is important to your success.* They probably know it, but it's nice to hear again.

Emotional Preparation

Even if you are entering basic training dreaming of becoming the toughest Guardian ever, you will still want to prepare yourself emotionally for the adventure on which you are about to embark. Begin by psyching yourself up during your time in the DEP.

- *Don't go in thinking that training will be too difficult.* You've prepared yourself during your time in the DEP, so you are ready for recruit training.
- *Enter basic training eager to learn.* Recruit training is all about learning the basics of being a Guardian. By the time you leave for training, you should be excited about spending all day

every day learning something new. That excitement will carry you through any rough patches.

- *Know that training is planned so as to give you the tools you need.* Every lesson you will learn in recruit training will prepare you for the next lesson. Pay attention and work hard and you *will* learn what you need to learn.
- *Remember that recruit training is not what life in the Coast Guard will be like every day.* Recruit training is only eight weeks long. You *can* get through it and then you will go on to enjoy being a Guardian.
- *Believe that you can succeed.* The Coast Guard selected you just as much as you selected them. They saw something in you; now you need to see it in yourself. If you want to be a Guardian and you work with that goal in mind, then you will succeed.

If you want to give yourself a lift while you are at recruit training, sit down and write yourself eight letters or postcards. In each one, remind yourself why you decided to become a Guardian, tell yourself that you are determined to succeed, and offer yourself encouraging words. You can slip in a photograph of a pet or your family or your friends; something that will make you smile when you see it. Stamp the letters or postcards and put a date on the outside of each one — one letter or postcard per week of basic training. Then give the letters to your recruiter, a parent, or a trusted friend and ask them to mail one to you each week while you are at basic training.

As your time in the DEP is drawing to a close, start looking towards the future. Soon you will leave for basic training and your journey to becoming a Guardian will begin. To give you an idea of what to expect during those eight weeks, the next chapter will tell you what happens in basic training, from the moment you arrive until the day you proudly graduate.

FOUR

Coast Guard
Basic Training

16

Overview

The goal of basic training is to take a civilian and turn him or her into a basic Guardian. Basic training is just that — the *basic* knowledge that new military members need to become a part of the Coast Guard. Recruits learn how to march, how to use a basic handgun, how to fight, how to maneuver in a variety of conditions, how to administer first aid and fight fires, how to read standard navigational aids, how to maneuver on a ship or boat, how to work as part of a team, as well as learning military and Coast Guard history, ethics, etiquette, customs, dress, etc.

Coast Guard basic training lasts for eight weeks, counting three days of paperwork and medical exams before basic training begins. Every day of the week is a training day, even Sundays, though recruits are allowed time for religious activities on Sunday mornings and they often get a break on Thanksgiving and Christmas. Recruits spend their days doing physical training, learning military skills (either in the classroom or hands on), and practicing what they've been taught. Training personnel make sure that even mundane activities like cleaning the squad-bay (dorm) are an opportunity for learning how to do things the military and Coast Guard way.

Coast Guard Basic Training Location

The Coast Guard trains recruits at only one location: Coast Guard Training Center, Cape May, NJ. Cape May has been part of military training and exercises since 1917 when the Navy established a base there. After World War I it was used by the Navy to test dirigibles — lighter-than-air ships — but after a crash the program was ended. The Coast

Guard began occupying the base in 1924 and the Navy officially turned it over to them in 1946. East Coast training was moved to Cape May in 1948 and in 1982 the Coast Guard moved all training operations to Cape May.

Between 4,000 and 5,000 recruits complete basic training at Cape May each year. The recruits are divided into companies of 80–100 recruits each. There are personnel who take care of all aspects of recruit training, from recruit receiving to medical attention to uniform and supply distribution. The Instructional Systems Branch is responsible for teaching the wide variety of basic training classes. In addition to recruit training, Cape May also houses the Coast Guard's Company Commander School and Recruiter School.

Recruit Company Commanders

Recruit Company Commanders are the main training personnel in charge of recruits. Usually each company of recruits has two company commanders. The Lead Company Commander oversees all aspects of his or her company's training and acts as a father or mother figure to the recruits, motivating them or challenging them as needed. The Company Commander acts as the "bad cop," the hard disciplinarian of the group, and is responsible for making sure recruits are ship-shape at all times. Overseeing the Lead Company Commander and the Company Commander are the Section Commander and the Battalion Commander.

Recruit Company Commanders are highly trained individuals. They are senior enlisted personnel who must complete an eight-week course that recreates every aspect of basic training. During their training, they learn how to motivate, instruct, and discipline. They must memorize all possible drill routines and be completely familiar with the standard operating procedures that Recruit Company Commanders must follow.

Guardians serve as Recruit Company Commanders for three years

Recruit Company Commanders are easily identified by their "Smokey the Bear" hat and their in-your-face teaching (Official U.S. Coast Guard photograph by Petty Officer 2nd Class Christopher D. McLaughlin).

and while they are in charge of a training company they can work upwards of 120 hours a week, on very little sleep and without seeing their families. They know how to do, and have done, everything that they tell recruits to do. When they are not overseeing a training company, they can accept a duty assignment to run classroom training or teach in other areas of basic training.

Gender Integrated Training

The Coast Guard trains male and female recruits together in integrated companies. (The Marine Corps is the only branch of the service that trains men and women separately.) Training for males and females is exactly the same, though a few of the female physical requirements are lighter. All recruits may have either male or female Company Commanders in charge of them during the day, but at night and in their squad bays, female recruits have female Company Commanders in charge of them. After basic training, there are no gender limitations on the jobs that male or female Guardians can do.

Training Schedule

The first three days at basic training is when new recruits receive their gear and undergo a series of medical and physical fitness tests to make sure they are ready for basic training. After that they are sent to their designated training company for recruit training.

Coast Guard basic training breaks down into distinct sections:

- *Arrival*: you get to Cape May, are issued gear, and are assigned to a company
- *Company Formation*: your company begins to learn how to work together and how to do things the Coast Guard way
- *Learning the Basics*: you learn the fundamentals of being a Guardian, such as terminology and military drill
- *Practical Training*: you begin to learn more about work in the Coast Guard, such as fighting fires, seamanship, and marksmanship
- *Preparation for your first unit*: as you get ready to join the fleet, you receive your first duty assignment; you continue to learn the practical skills you will need there
- *Graduation*: you finish Coast Guard basic training and leave to begin your work as a Guardian

Those first few weeks are when the Recruit Company Commanders are hardest on you. As you begin to progress through recruit training and show that you can handle the responsibilities of being a future

Guardian, you'll be given more opportunity to work on your own and to show leadership and initiative. By the time graduation arrives, you'll be familiar with the basics you need to be a Guardian. After graduation, new Guardians get five days of leave and then they are sent to their first duty station.

17

Basic Training Tips

Coast Guard basic training is designed to break down you as a civilian and remake you into a Guardian. But this process cannot happen without your help. That means that in order to succeed in basic training you have to *decide* that you are going to succeed. There are things you can do that will help ensure you have a successful time in basic training.

- *Adjust your attitude.* You might be the best student in your school or the toughest person in your neighborhood, but the moment you set foot on Coast Guard Training Center Cape May you become the lowest rung of the ladder. You are only a Seaman Recruit. High and mighty attitudes and chips on your shoulder have no place in recruit training, not with your company commanders and not with your fellow recruits.
- *Accept the loss of freedom.* You will have to do what the military says; there is no way to get around that. Fighting the system will only frustrate you. Instead accept that you are giving up some freedoms and remind yourself of what you are receiving in return. After all, even if you stayed a civilian and got a job in an office or a factory or a store, you would still have to bend to the rules of your organization.
- *Don't take things personally.* Company commanders are going to yell, but they don't do it because they hate you. They do this to see how you handle yourself when you are under stress. Life at sea can be stressful and the Coast Guard needs personnel who can keep going even when tired and harassed. Know that the yelling and the other stresses are not directed at you per-

sonally and know that learning to handle them will make you a stronger person.

- *Don't be lazy and don't give up.* Company commanders want recruits who work hard, try their best, and don't quit. Nothing will make them mad faster than laziness or recruits who stop before giving everything they can. If they think you can keep going, then you can. Ignore the voice in your head telling you to stop. Persevere. You'll be surprised by how much you can accomplish.

- *Don't show off.* Just as you don't want to give up too soon, you also don't want to always strive to beat everyone around you. That is not the sign of a good leader or a good teammate and the Coast Guard wants recruits who can be both. The only person you are competing with is yourself. Be the best *you* can be at everything you are assigned and don't worry about trying to outdo your fellow recruits. Basic training is about what *you* can accomplish. Those recruits who excel and win awards are the ones who aren't trying for acclaim. They are simply doing their very best every single day of training.

- *Do what you are told, when you are told, and how you are told—without question.* In a combat situation there is not time to question orders. Your company commanders are preparing you for that now by expecting you to immediately obey every order — no matter how bizarre or impossible — without questioning. The sooner you learn to do this, the easier time you'll have during recruit training.

- *Tell the truth and do not make excuses.* NEVER lie to your company commanders for any reason. They will know that you lied and they will make your life harder because of it. If you made a mistake, admit to it, but don't try to explain why. If you don't know the answer, admit to it. Your life will be much easier if you keep things honest and if you don't try to justify your actions.

- *Pay close attention. Pay especially close attention to safety issues.* No matter how tired you are, pay attention to everything your company commanders say. Often they will be giving you hints (or even outright telling you) about what you can expect during training or the best way to complete an exercise. Pay even closer attention when they are talking about safety. The military takes safety very seriously, especially during training. Nothing will get you in trouble faster than ignoring or forgetting instructions.

- *Encourage teamwork.* Teamwork is paramount to military life. The Coast Guard will expect you to immediately work as a team with your fellow recruits. Your company commanders will not care if you don't like someone. In fact, not liking them makes it even more likely that you will be forced to work together! The faster you and your fellow recruits learn to work together — during training, in the squad-bay, and in the classroom — the better your basic training experience will be.

- *Look out for your fellow Guardians.* You will learn that the Guardians work as a team at all times. This philosophy begins in basic training. Whenever possible, help out your fellow recruits and they, in turn, will help you.

- *Deal with differences maturely.* Your fellow recruits will be from all parts of the country, all types of backgrounds, all ages, all levels of education, and all political and religious beliefs. It is your responsibility to be respectful of those differences. That doesn't mean you have to like all of your fellow recruits and it doesn't mean you can resort to violence to "get them in line"; it means you have to find a way to interact like mature adults. Focus on the mission at hand and you will soon find that differences don't matter as much as teamwork.

- *Be the type of leader you would want to follow.* The Coast Guard wants its Guardians to be leaders, but being a leader doesn't mean that you are bossy or mean or that you look down on those below you. Think about the kind of leader you respect. What does he or she do that makes them a good leader? That is the type of person you should strive to be when you are placed in a leadership role, both during basic training and after.

- *Take every opportunity to learn from those around you.* You will be amazing how much you will learn just from watching your fellow recruits, your company commanders, and the other personnel you encounter. Go into basic training believing that every person you meet will teach you something and be eager to accept those lessons.

- *Make friends.* The Coast Guard is a small service. You are training with the people who will one day stand beside you on board ship. Get to know them, ask about their background and interests and reasons for enlisting, find out who they are. Having friends will make your time in basic training a shared experience rather than a solo survival expedition.

- *Take care of your body.* Injuries and illnesses will, at best, make training harder. At the worst, they could cause you to be set back in training or even put an end to training all together. Drink plenty of water. Keep your nails clipped, powder your feet, and tend to blisters. Wash your hands regularly, especially before eating or after going to the bathroom. If you hurt yourself or think you are sick, tell your company commander immediately, no matter how fearsome he or she is. Company commanders are trained both to spot fakers and to see the signs of serious injury or illness, so he or she will know if you are well enough to continue training or if you need to visit a doctor.

- *Use "free time" to your advantage.* You won't get a lot of time to yourself, but you will get some and that time can help you recharge and regroup. Use free time to study, write letters to friends and family, and get to know your fellow recruits.

- *Develop a military bearing.* No matter what the situation, no matter how much you are being yelled at, no matter whose fault a problem is, you need to remain calm, collected, and mature. Don't whine, try to explain, or display emotions. If you act like you are calm and rational, then you will soon be calm and rational, even when you are faced with combat stresses. Learn to let distractions — from cold winds to company commanders in your face to tiredness in class — roll off your back.

- *Ask for help if you need it.* If you are injured, sick, or if you begin to have suicidal thoughts, you must ask for help immediately. Do not allow fear of your company commander or of getting set back to keep you from getting the help you need. It is more important that you treat the problem up front, before it becomes a much bigger issue. Likewise, if you are having trouble understanding some aspect of training, ask your fellow trainees to help you study. They are likely to appreciate the chance to help you, especially since it means they'll be getting in valuable studying at the same time.

- *Remember that basic training is NOT what life in the military is like.* The goal of Coast Guard recruit training is to turn you from a civilian into a Guardian. Your company commanders do this by breaking you down and then rebuilding you. After you graduate successfully from basic training, you will still have to work hard and remain professional, but you will not be faced with the same deprivations and strictures that you must live with during basic training.

- *Keep a positive attitude.* This can be hard, especially when you are feeling frustrated, tired, sore, discouraged, and/or homesick, but you have to stay positive. Think of each day as a new chance to try your hardest. Focus on the short term goal of getting through one day at a time and don't forget the long term goal or goals that led you to join the Coast Guard. Remember that thousands of men and women have gone through basic training successfully and you can too. At the end of each day, remind yourself of at least one good thing you accomplished that day and begin to look forward to the next day as another opportunity to learn. Each day is one day closer to you becoming a Guardian!

Leaving for Basic Training

During the weeks you've spent in the Delayed Entry Program, you've been working hard to get ready to leave for basic training. You should now be excited and eager and, most of all, ready to begin your new journey.

Final Preparations

As the time draws closer for you to leave for basic training, your recruiter will meet with you to go over your paperwork again. Make sure that everything is correct. Once you get to basic training, you will not be able to make changes. If something is not in your enlistment contract — whether it be a promotion, a bonus, or something else — then it doesn't exist. Read your contract carefully and make sure changes are made as soon as needed.

You will go back to the Military Entrance Processing Station (MEPS) to complete your paperwork, get reexamined by the doctors to make sure any medical issues have not arisen since your last visit, and to take the final Oath of Enlistment. Your recruiter will also make sure that nothing has happened to change your eligibility. During your time in the Delayed Entry Program you should have been keeping your recruiter apprised of any problems or changes that might affect your eligibility. It is better to address such issues now rather than wait until basic training. Once you take the final Oath of Enlistment and ship to basic training, you are bound by the Uniform Code of

Military Justice and are subject to court-martial if you break military law.

After your recruiter has gone over your paperwork and after the doctors have looked you over again, then you will be discharged from the Delayed Entry Program. You then take the Oath of Enlistment for the second and final time. (If you are enlisting as a reservist, then you will not need to take the Oath again. You became a part of the military as soon as you took the Oath the first time.) As mentioned in Chapter 12: Visiting the Military Entrance Processing Station (MEPS), the Oath of Enlistment is a serious, solemn vow. You should not take it lightly. Read over it once more and make sure you are able to agree to it, freely and clearly.

> *I, _____, do solemnly swear (or affirm) that I will support and defend the Constitution of the United States against all enemies, foreign and domestic; that I will bear true faith and allegiance to the same; and that I will obey the orders of the President of the United States and the orders of the officers appointed over me, according to regulations and the Uniform Code of Military Justice. So help me God.*

Family members are welcome to attend your swearing of the Oath. After the ceremony is over, you should say good-bye to them, because you'll be leaving for basic training and they will not be able to go with you past this point.

Your travel to basic training will be arranged for you. Your recruiter will make sure that you know where you need to go and how you are getting there, whether you are traveling by bus or plane and whether or not you need to spend the night anywhere. All of your travel to basic training is paid for, as are any meals or hotel visits.

Packing for the Journey

Each branch of the military will give you a list of what to bring with you to basic training. The Coast Guard says you should bring with you ONLY:

- *Your wallet and any needed documents*: your Social Security Card, your driver's license or picture ID, your permanent resident alien/ green card (if applicable), and any other paperwork or documents your recruiter gives you or tells you to bring (such as your marriage certificate, your child/children's birth certificate(s), etc.)
- *Prescription medicines*: also bring a paper copy of the prescription from your doctor; this is assuming that the medicines have already been approved by the doctors at MEPS
- *Eyeglasses and contact lenses*: bring both even if you normally only wear contacts
- *Fifty dollars in cash*
- *Pre-paid phone card*
- *Your recruiter's business card*
- *Wedding band* (if applicable)
- *Religious material* (if applicable): a medallion on a chain long enough to hide under a v-neck t-shirt, a Bible, and/or a religious reference book
- *Small address book*: with your family and friends' contact information
- *Stationery and stamps*: if you go ahead and address and stamp the envelopes before you leave home, that will save you time later
- *Photos*: two, wallet-sized only; nothing pornographic
- *Watch*: one that is waterproof, non-descript, and has a second hand is best
- *Small duffel bag*: bring a bag clearly marked with your name on the outside; this will be used to store your civilian clothes until after graduation
- *Toiletries*
  - All recruits should bring:
    - *Razor, shaving cream, shaving kit*: only bring safety-type razors, not straight or electric
    - *Lotion*: Unscented
    - *Talcum powder*
    - *Toothbrush*

- ° Female recruits should also bring:
  - *Hair care items*: portable blow-dryer; elastics which match your hair color; bobby pins and barrettes in gold, silver, or a color that matches your hair
  - *Makeup*: minimal amounts and it should be neutral in color (makeup is for graduation, photos, and off-base liberty only)
  - *Feminine hygiene items*: If it is your time of the month, you can bring supplies with you, but you do not need to bring enough for all of basic training, as you will have the opportunity to purchase more once you are issued supplies.
- *Clothing*
  - ° All recruits should bring:
    - *T-Shirts*: three white v-neck shirts
    - *Underwear*: six to ten pairs of white underpants (not thongs)
    - *Long underwear*: dark blue or black; only for those recruits training between October and April
  - ° Female recruits should also bring:
    - *Pantyhose*: 1 pair of skin-toned hose
    - *Bras*: 6 white or skin-tone sports bras (be sure they are supportive enough for running)
    - *Half-slip*: 1 white or skin-tone
    - *Earrings*: 1 set of gold, silver, pearl, or diamond ball earrings (earrings are for graduation, photos, and off-base liberty only)

You should not bring any weapons, playing cards, dice, pornography, food, gum, tobacco products, alcohol, illegal drugs, over-the-counter drugs (not even aspirin), jewelry (except for a wedding ring and/or a religious necklace, and a small set of earrings if you are female), electronic devices (such as MP3 players or video game consoles), cameras, nail polish, large amounts of money, or any valuables.

Please note that your recruiter will give you the latest list of what you can and cannot bring with you to basic training. Follow that list exactly. It will save you a lot of hassle and insure that you are not singled out by the company commanders when you first get to training.

If you must bring a cellphone with you while you travel, it will be stored while you are in basic training. (BE SURE to turn it off as soon as you get on the bus to travel to the training center.) You can bring a book or magazine with you if you need something to keep you occupied during your travels, but leave it at the airport or bus station for future passengers to enjoy. Since you don't need to bring much with you, leave large bags and purses at home. Bring a bag small enough to carry just your needed supplies.

You'll want to wear comfortable clothes for your journey, but make sure they look neat and professional. Khaki slacks with a polo or long sleeve shirt are good choices. Try to wear pants with pockets because you'll need a place to hold a pen and other items once you get to recruit training. Roll down your sleeves, tuck in your shirt, and button your top collar button as soon as you get on the bus to the recruit training depot. You will be on your feet a lot, so wear shoes that support your feet. Closed-toe shoes with socks are best. Do not wear any earrings or nail polish. You do not want to stand out in any way when you arrive because that will guarantee that you will be harassed by instructors. Instead, aim to look bland and professional. Cape May can be cold, so it is appropriate to wear a warm coat and/or a sweater in the winter.

Men do not need to get a haircut before leaving for basic training (your head will be shaved soon enough!), but you should make sure your hair looks tidy. Women do not need to get their hair cut before training, even though they won't be getting their head shaved. But during training you'll need to keep your hair up and off your collar, so a shorter, easy to manage cut is a good idea. Before arriving at training, female recruits should put their hair into a bun or other neat hairstyle that keeps the hair off of their collar.

During Your Travels

Depending on where you are coming from, you may travel by van, bus, or airplane in order to get to basic training. Your recruiter will make sure you have all of the information and tickets you need to get to where you are going. If you live close enough where you do not have to fly, then you probably won't need a meal voucher. (Sometimes, though, kindly bus drivers will stop to allow new recruits to get one last fast food meal before they get to training.)

If you are coming from farther away, then you will fly into Philadelphia and take a bus or van from there. More than likely you'll get a meal voucher to spend at the airport. Be sure to throw away any leftover snacks or drinks before you get to basic training. You aren't allowed to bring them with you to the Training Center.

You may be the only person from your town or region heading to basic training, but you'll meet up with other recruits soon enough. These are the men and women you'll be training alongside, so be friendly and approachable. If there is a group of recruits traveling together, MEPS or your recruiter will appoint one recruit as a leader of the small group. It is the leader's job to make sure everyone gets to where they are supposed to be, when they are supposed to be there. The leader is also in charge of the group's official paperwork and must keep control of that paperwork at all times.

If you get separated from the group when traveling by air or if you run into any other problems, ask airport personnel to direct you to the nearest USO (United Service Organizations) office. There is usually a USO office in every airport and the personnel there can get you back on track. Otherwise, call your recruiter and explain the situation to him or her.

The United States Military Entrance Processing Command — the department that oversees all MEPS locations — has a video which explains recruit travel to basic training. It is particularly useful if you have never flown before, as it outlines all of the procedures for navigating through an airport. You can watch the video here: *http://www.mepcom. army.mil/travel-video.html*.

When you get to the Philadelphia airport, before you leave on the bus for Cape May, you should call your family to let them know that you arrived. You will not have a chance to call them until roughly week five of basic training, so this will be your last opportunity to talk to them for some time.

As mentioned before, you can bring a book or magazine to read while you are traveling and you should try to meet some of the other new recruits with whom you're traveling. But the most important thing you can do during your travels from home to recruit training is to rest. The first days at recruit training are long and sleepless and overwhelming. You will want to get as much rest beforehand as you can. All too soon your bus will be pulling into Cape May and your civilian life will end as your new military life begins.

19

Arrival

The main part of Coast Guard basic training is seven and a half weeks long, but you will be at Cape May for eight weeks all total. The first few days are called Arrival. That is the time when you are processed into the Coast Guard. How long you stay there depends on when you arrive at basic training. While there you will fill out paperwork, get medical checkups, receive your gear, and finally, at the end, be added to a company and picked up by your company commanders. After your company commanders pick up your new company, they will spend the first few days indoctrinating you into the Coast Guard — teaching you the basics of how to march, talk, and think like a Guardian — as well as learning personal information about each of you, finishing up administrative details, transferring you to your new squad bay, etc.

The arrival days can in many ways be more stressful than the rest of basic training. You are confused, tired, homesick, and, most of all, afraid you have made a terrible mistake. To make it worse, there is a lot of "hurry up and wait," so you have time to worry about what you've gotten yourself into. But don't let yourself get down. Focus on how each part of the process brings you one step closer to being a Guardian. Now is not the time to decide you do not want to go through basic training. You are here and you must continue. Failure to train will only set you up for extra attention by your company commanders, never a good thing.

Arriving at Basic Training

The Coast Guard personnel who oversee Arrival must be highly organized in order to process the high number of recruits who arrive in the early days of each week. The staff at Cape May will get a call from the Coast Guard liaisons who are escorting recruits at the airport and other transportation stations with a head count, so that they know in advance how many recruits are arriving, when they will arrive, and their gender breakdown. When the bus carrying the new recruits passes through the gates at Cape May, the personnel at the gate call so that the company commanders in charge of greeting the arrivals can be ready to get things started.

You will arrive at the recruit training center on a Tuesday evening. When you arrive depends upon where you are traveling from and whether or not you have to wait for other recruits to join you. Since the Coast Guard is such a small service, you will probably have to do some waiting at the airport for other recruits to arrive, so that there are enough of you to fill a bus, but if you live close to Cape May, then you might be assigned to arrive via passenger van. Either way, all new arrivals receive the same treatment. As soon as your bus or van pulls up to Sexton Hall, a company commander will step on board and begin loudly

Nervous new recruits arrive at Cape May to begin basic training (Official U.S. Coast Guard photograph by Petty Officer Christopher D. McLaughlin).

informing you that you 15 seconds to get off the vehicle and line up on a series of yellow triangles painted on the asphalt, men separated from women, "and you've just wasted 10 of them." The triangles are designed to put you in proper body position for attention. The company commander will tell you to place your hands at your sides, with any bags at your feet. If you have not already done so, you will be instructed to roll down your sleeves, tuck in your shirt, and button your top collar button. Women will be told to pull their hair up off of their collar into a bun.

While you are standing at attention on the footprints, the drill instructor will tell you that you are now a Coast Guard recruit and that as such you are to do what you are told, when you are told to do it, exactly as you are told to do it, without question. Then you will be marched inside to begin processing.

The First Night

Your first night at basic training will probably pass in a blur. You will do a lot of paperwork and there is also a lot of waiting. Your job during those hours is to listen, closely and carefully. There will be a lot of yelling, but if you pay attention and don't panic, then you will get through without too much trouble. If you have "free time," then study the Recruit Training Pocket Guide that you will be issued almost immediately. It contains all of the information that you need to know to graduate, so the sooner you learn that information, the better off you'll be. The Recruit Training Pocket Guide can be found online at *http://www.uscg.mil/hq/capemay/docs/RecruitTrainingPocket Guide.pdf.*

You will not be able to call home to let your family know that you have arrived, but a letter will be sent out to them from the administration at Cape May. The letter will let them know that you have arrived, what your mailing address is, and that you will contact them closer to graduation to give them details on the graduation ceremony.

In the beginning, you'll mostly be filling out paperwork. As soon as you enter Sexton Hall, you will head to what looks like a classroom, complete with either tables or individual desks. You will be given paperwork to fill out and you will be told exactly how to fill it out. Do not fill in any information until you are told. Write only what you are told to write and do it as soon as you are told to do it. Over the course of the evening, you will fill out a lot of paperwork and some of it may seem repetitive, but it is all vital to getting you processed into the Coast Guard. The paperwork is important and will insure that you are properly processed, but — as with many things in basic training — it is also a way for the Coast Guard to get you used to following orders. One vital piece of information will be your recruit company designation. You should memorize this as soon as you are told it.

This first evening is also when you will turn in your personal effects, meaning the civilian clothes you arrived in, your cellphone, and other items which can be returned to you after training. You should not have brought much with you. (See Chapter 18 for a list of items to bring.) There will be a "Moment of Truth" where you can turn in any contraband, such as weapons, pornography, prescription drugs, etc. The Moment of Truth also allows you to confess to anything that you might not have told your recruiter about, such as a medical ailment like asthma or a minor criminal conviction. Ideally you will not have anything to report, since you will not have lied to your recruiter or omitted information. Lying during the Moment of Truth will not work as a way of getting out of basic training. The Coast Guard will be verifying anything you tell them and if they find that there is nothing preventing you from beginning training, then you *will* be beginning training. If your information is double-checked and it shows that you are ineligible for training, then you will begin processing to be sent back home.

After turning in your personal effects, you will change into your first uniform: Coast Guard t-shirts, sweatpants, and running shoes. You will be fed a boxed meal and shown to a temporary squad bay. By this time it will be around 1 A.M., but you won't get much sleep.

Instead a screaming company commander will wake you up at 5 A.M. by to continue the process of entering into Coast Guard recruit training.

The Next Few Days

Much of the rest of Arrival is taken up with medical testing. The doctors at basic training will put you through the same tests and evaluations that you underwent at MEPS. This is to ensure that any issues are caught before you begin training. It is important to remember that the doctors and nurses are not trying to disqualify you on purpose. They are only thinking of the greater good. What can be a simple problem for a civilian can be a major one for someone undergoing the rigors of military training. The medical personnel not only have to consider your safety and health, they have to consider how your physical issues will affect the units with which you will serve.

You will be drug tested again, so it should go without saying that you will not have been using any illegal drugs at any time before arriving at basic training. Female recruits will be tested for pregnancy and all recruits will be tested for sexually transmitted diseases. Additionally, you will visit the dentist who will evaluate your teeth and do any needed dental work. You will also visit an eye doctor who will check your eyes, verify your prescription (if you wear glasses or contacts), and issue you new, military-style glasses.

If major problems are found during your medical exams — problems which will prevent you from continuing training — you will be processed out of the Coast Guard. Unfortunately that is the end of your military career, unless the issue is a temporary one which will clear up in a matter of months.

You will also begin receiving your gear. There is a lot of gear given to you during basic training and you are expected to account for it. Some of your gear is yours permanently and you are charged for it. The charges come directly out of your paycheck, so you don't need to have money with you. Other gear is only yours temporarily while you are training and you will have to return it. You will be issued everything from uniforms (including outerwear, socks, shoes, hats, and belts) to school supplies (a guidebook of essential information, notebooks, pens and pencils) to hygiene items (shampoo, laundry detergent, soap, toothpaste, towels, etc.) to military supplies (packs, canteens, etc.), to miscellaneous items like combination locks. Two days after you arrive you will finally get your work clothes, call ODUs, or operational dress uniforms.

The infamous haircuts are given during Arrival. All male recruits will have their heads shaved. This is done quickly by a team of civilian barbers and soon all the male recruits have the same hairstyle. Female recruits do not have their hair cut. They should arrive at the recruit training facility with their hair already neat and up off of their collar.

In addition to filling out paperwork, getting gear issued to you, and undergoing medical evaluations, during your three to five days in Arrival you will learn how to make up your bed ("rack") in military fashion, learn how to address company commanders, and possibly even learn some basics of how to march. You will probably stand a watch (aka: do guard duty) during the night and you will start getting used to following directions quickly and correctly. Soon it will be time for you to meet the company commanders who will be in charge of you for the next seven and a half weeks.

Joining a Company

On Friday afternoon you will finally be done with your medical exams and your paperwork. At that point you will be assigned to your company, a group of about 80 to 100 men and women with whom you will train. At this point you will also meet your company commanders and they will move you over to the squad bay where you will live during recruit training.

Indoctrination Weekend

The first weekend that you are with your company commanders is called Indoctrination Weekend. The goal of Indoctrination Weekend is to shock you into paying attention. There is a lot of yelling and a lot of physical activity. You will feel like you cannot do anything right. That is the point. Your company commanders want you to feel like you are falling apart so that they can be the ones to put you back together as a Guardian. As part of this, your company commanders will introduce you to "incentive training," physical activity used to punish you for not following orders, not doing something correctly, etc. You will probably also have a fire drill or some other simulated emergency, just to keep you off-balance.

Also during this time, your company commanders will learn about

Incentive training will get you in shape, but it's not supposed to be fun! (Official U.S. Coast Guard photograph by Petty Officer Christopher D. McLaughlin).

their new company. They need to know who is left-handed, who is a reservist, what religions are represented, etc. They will make sure that you have all of your gear and that all your paperwork has been filled out and added to your file. They will get the company settled into the squad bay and make sure that you know how to store your gear, make up your rack, and do what you're told to do.

For your part, you will begin to learn the basics of how to drill, how to wear your uniform, etc.—everything you need to know to understand basic training. You will attend your first religious services (if you so desire) on Sunday. By Monday your company will be finished with Indoctrination and ready to begin full basic training the next day.

Life During
Basic Training

The schedule for what happens when during basic training only tells part of the story. You're probably still wondering about the basic, day-to-day aspects of boot camp life. No one can completely prepare you for what you'll experience during basic training, because every recruit's time at basic training is different, but the general details remain the same for all enlistees.

Addressing Your Recruit Company Commanders

Every branch of the service has a different way that recruit training instructors should be addressed. In the Coast Guard, during the first week of training, you will address your company commander as "sir" or "ma'am." After the second week, when you have learned Coast Guard ranks, you will then address your company commanders and all other instructors by their proper rank (i.e. "Petty Officer Smith"). Once you make the switch, you should never use "sir" or "ma'am" to address any enlisted instructors or company commanders. While addressing your company commanders, you should look forward. Never stare them directly in the eyes. You have not yet earned that right.

Discipline and Punishment

Many people assume that company commanders can curse at, hit, bully, and abuse their recruits, but that is no longer the case. That does

Recruit Company Commanders work together to make sure that training is effective and unforgettable (Official U.S. Coast Guard photograph by Lt. j.g. Michael Cole).

not mean, however, that company commanders have become gentle teddy bears. They are still allowed to "motivate" you, using a combination of yelling and physical activity. Company commanders are taught how to motivate using a loud, powerful voice. You will quickly learn to listen to everything they are saying, because you want to be able to do what they want when they want it.

One unique aspect of the Coast Guard is the use of performance trackers. Performance trackers are like demerit forms. You will be required to carry two of them with you at all times. Any time you violate the standards you should be upholding, the company commander or instructor who saw the infraction will have you hand over a performance tracker. He or she will fill out the tracker with the details and the tracker will be given to your company commander who will make the decision about appropriate punishment.

If you don't do what you are supposed to or if you get a performance tracker pulled, then you'll most likely be disciplined using physical exercises, called Incentive Training. Company commanders have clear guidelines on what physical activities may be used during Incentive Training to motivate and discipline recruits. Other acceptable punishments include removing your free time or assigning you to do guard duty (waking up for an hour to keep watch while the other recruits sleep). Regularly not doing what you are supposed to and/or having too many performance trackers pulled could land you in the Recruit Aptitude Motivational Program and/or get you reverted.

You *will* experience some form of discipline during your time in recruit training, whether it is because you did something wrong or because your whole platoon messed up or because one person messed up and your company commander decided to make a point by punishing everyone. Whichever it is, know that it is coming and take it like a Guardian.

Food and Sleep

You'll be so active during basic training that food and sleep may be two of your major concerns. Recruits are guaranteed seven to eight full hours of sleep a night — with a few exceptions. When you are keeping watch or if your company does night training exercises, your sleep time may be cut down by an hour or so. During training you'll get three meals per day. These meals may be eaten in the dining facility, where you'll have a choice of hot foods and drinks. You aren't given much time to eat — about 20 minutes — and you are not allowed to talk during the meal. Eat a balanced meal of proteins, vegetables, and carbohydrates, because you'll need the energy. Try to avoid sweets which will not stick with you between meals. During the summer months, you'll want to add extra salt to your food to replace the salt you lose through sweating.

Company commanders no longer force recruits to drink massive amounts of water, since too much water is as bad for you as too little. Instead, you'll be issued a canteen and you'll have plenty of opportunities to refill it. In most of the restrooms you'll find a urine color chart. The chart shows you what color your urine should be if you are well-hydrated. (An example can be found here: *http://www.nmcphc.med.navy.mil/down loads/healthyliv/nutrition/urinekleurenkaart.pdf.*)

Free Time

Free time is time when you can study, read your mail, write letters, take care of personal issues, etc. During free time there will be a company commander on duty and you can consult with him or her, but he or she will not be leading any instruction. You have the right to one hour of free time per day on Mondays through Saturdays and roughly five hours on Sunday mornings and holidays, but you won't always get that full amount. It can be curtailed as a discipline or because training interrupts or other because of other issues. Overall, though, you will get free time every day and if your company has been especially good, your company may be generous and give you time on a Saturday.

Graduation Requirements

In order to graduate from Coast Guard basic training, you must meet the following requirements:

- Pass written and practical exams from all classes
- Pass swim assessment
- Pass physical fitness assessment
- Prove your proficiency in and familiarity with firefighting, first aid, CPR, firearms, basic aids to navigation, and lookout and helmsman duties

Housing

Recruits live in squad-bays. Squad-bays are a lot like dorms, except that you're sharing with a company of men or women instead of just one roommate! You'll sleep in bunk beds, arranged head-to-feet, meaning the feet of recruit in the top bunk are above the head of the recruit in the bottom bunk. The recruits in the bunk beds on either side are arranged in the opposite way. This helps prevent the spread of disease. One of the very first things you will learn is how to make a bed the military way — and how to do it quickly.

Each recruit has his or her own storage space in the squad-bay. Company commanders will teach you how to arrange your belongings in a military manner. You are expected to maintain your storage space and your belongings at all times. This is practice for when you are assigned to living quarters on board a ship. These quarters are small and each person in them needs to keep his or her belongings organized, so that they do not affect the other crewmembers' use of the same space.

Recruits are responsible for cleaning the squad-bay, the bathrooms, and the company commanders' areas. Your company commanders will look for dirt in the smallest of places, such as over the top of a window or a door. If they find it, then your whole company is likely to be disciplined.

Hygiene

You are given time each day to take care of personal hygiene, but not a lot of time. You'll learn the fast, Coast Guard way of taking a shower, shaving, going to the bathroom, brushing your teeth, and getting dressed each morning. And you'll do it all in front of everyone in your squad-bay. There are no private bathrooms in basic training; showers and sinks are communal. But you'll be hurrying too much to worry about being shy.

Female recruits may not have enough time to shave their legs. Company commanders sometimes don't give you enough time on purpose; nicks and cuts on freshly shaved legs can quickly become infected by grime picked up during training. But company commanders will give their recruits time to shave their legs before graduation or inspections or liberty time.

There are bathrooms in classroom areas, as well as in the squad-bay. Company commanders give recruits plenty of opportunities to use them, so you'll never need to worry about finding one when you need it. Female recruits may not get their periods during training because of the high level of activity and stress, but if they do, they simply carry supplies with them throughout the day. Supplies can be purchased at the Exchange as needed.

Male recruits have their heads shaved during Arrival. They will visit the barbers each week for a trim. All of those haircuts are subtracted from their pay. Female recruits do not have their heads shaved, but they are expected to maintain neat and tidy hairstyles that keep the hair so that 2 inches or less is on their neck. Women may have short hair, they may keep their hair in a bun, or they may have short, tight cornrows or similar styles. The important thing to remember is that any hairstyle you have must be able to be maintained neatly at all times, even when you are taking your "cover" (your hat) on and off, and there is not a lot of time at night for fixing complicated braids. (Something to keep in mind — if you have your hair in a bun, you are slightly more anonymous since that is how many female Guardians wear their hair. That can be good for staying below the radar.)

The combination of lots of people, high stress, and the sweat and dirt of training means that you have to be extra careful to remain healthy during basic training. Remember to wash your hands after using the restroom and before eating in order to prevent the spread of disease. Do not share combs, brushes, personal grooming tools, canteens, etc. with your fellow recruits. Make sure you work hard to keep the squad-bay as clean as possible.

Leadership Roles and Recruit Jobs

The Coast Guard wants recruits to begin learning and practicing leading immediately, so there are a number of leadership positions that recruits can volunteer for or be assigned to. Whether you must volunteer or if you will simply be assigned to a leadership role is usually up to the whim of the company commander. The Coast Guard offers recruits the chance to be a Recruit Petty Officer or RPO. The RPOs are the recruits who are in charge of the other recruits, especially when the company commanders are not around. There is often a Recruit Chief Petty Officer and one or two RPOs under him or her.

You should know, though, that being a leader during basic training does put you in the spotlight and that means that you will be more closely scrutinized by company commanders. It is not uncommon for recruit leaders to be disciplined when one of the recruits they are in charge of messes up or if the company commander does not think that the recruit leader has done a good job. Recruit leaders are often "fired" from their positions, but try not to take it personally. This is partially done to add to the stress of recruit training, but also to allow other recruits to have a chance to assume a leadership role.

There are also jobs — called billets — which are given to specific recruits. These jobs include:

- Division Laundry Petty Officer: makes sure laundry is correctly processed for the cleaners
- Recruit Athletic Petty Officer: makes sure the company's recruits are ready for their physical fitness assessment
- Recruit Damage Control Petty Officer: makes sure all fire extinguishers are kept up-to-date and ready to use
- Recruit Mail Petty Officer: picks up and delivers the company's mail
- Recruit Medical Yeoman and Recruit Dental Yeoman: help the company commander keep track of the medical and dental records for the company, as well as scheduling medical and dental appointments

Playing in the recruit Ceremonial Band will give you a chance to support your fellow recruits at graduation and other ceremonies (Official U.S. Coast Guard photograph by Lt. j.g. Michael Cole).

- Recruit Religious Petty Officer: company's religious leader, makes sure all recruits have a chance to practice their religion
- Recruit Yeoman: secretary of the company, takes notes and keeps logs

There is a recruit Ceremonial Band on Cape May. If you play an instrument and/or have marching band experience, you can apply to be a part of the band. The Ceremonial Band plays at Graduation and at other Coast Guard events around Cape May.

Recruit Aptitude Motivational Program (RAMP) and Reverting or Getting Set Back

The Recruit Aptitude Motivational Program (or RAMP) is a uniquely Coast Guard institution. The goal of RAMP is to take recruits who are under-motivated — those who aren't showing the proper work ethic or who keep getting in trouble — and turn them into recruits who are more engaged in and committed to training. While in the RAMP, you are only guaranteed four hours of sleep and the rest of your time is spent in Incentive Training — aka, physical exercise — as well as motivational speeches and classes meant to show you that you should work harder and appreciate the opportunity to become a member of the Coast Guard. Recruits will usually spend about three or four days in RAMP before being rejoining a company.

When you are reverted or set back in training, you are moved to another recruit training company that is not as far along in training as the group you are currently assigned to. This can happen for a number of reasons. Sometimes it occurs for disciplinary reasons, because you have not followed instructions, have too many performance trackers pulled, or have caused a serious violation. Time spent in RAMP can often cause you to be reverted.

Other times reverting is done because you have not met the academic or physical standards that you need to in order to progress in training. If you fail a test or do not qualify in swimming, then you can be set back to give you time to learn the skills you need to graduate. Reverting can also occur if you are injured or become seriously ill. For example, if you sprain your ankle during training, you will be given time to heal and then, because your training unit will have continued without you, you will be placed into a training unit that is at the same point in their training as you were when you were injured.

Religious Services

As the smallest of the services, the Coast Guard does not have its own corps of chaplains. Instead the Navy provides chaplains and religious services for the Coast Guard. Coast Guard recruits come from a wide variety of religious backgrounds and the Coast Guard tries hard to make sure that all of their recruits are able to practice their faith.

During the time when your company commander is getting to know his or her company, you will be asked what religion you are. That will give them the information they need to plan for your religious needs. However, due to the demands of training, not all aspects of religious worship (such as Friday or Saturday services, special religious meals, or other religious requirements) may be able to be accommodated.

All religious services take place on Sunday mornings between 8 A.M. and 1 P.M., regardless of the religion. The chapel on Cape May offers a Catholic service and a Protestant Christian service. Recruits who are Jewish, Latter Day Saints, Greek Orthodox, and Seventh-Day Adventist can go to services in the local community. Recruits who are Buddhist, Muslim, Hindu, Wiccan, and other religions may have the opportunity to attend services led by volunteers from the local community, but it depends on whether there is a group in Cape May able to accommodate you.

You are not required to attend religious services. If you do not currently practice any religion or if you are atheist, you can remain in the squad-bay during Sunday services. Or you are welcome to visit different religious services to learn more about various faiths. Some recruits attend services simply for the quiet and the break from training. On Sundays and during the week, chaplains are available to counsel recruits who are having trouble with some aspect of recruit training. Additionally, two recruits from each company will be assigned to be Company Religious Representatives, responsible for helping meet the religious needs of the recruits in their company.

Safety, Injuries, and Illness

The personnel in charge of basic training are very careful to make it as safe as possible, even for a training regimen that involves firefighting! Company commander training includes CPR, early detection of medical problems, suicide prevention, stress management, counseling techniques, and more. At every training location there are personnel to act as spotters and to assist recruits when needed. During swim qualifications, there are specially trained instructors who are familiar with every aspect of water safety and survival. As the Coast Guard is a small service, it does not have its own medical personnel. Instead the Navy provides medical care for the Coast Guard. Navy corpsmen (medical personnel) are on hand to treat injuries and illnesses and there are Navy doctors and nurses stationed at the base hospital to treat more serious problems. Recruits are continually taught safety procedures, whether they are learning to swim, learning seamanship, or learning how to fire weapons. Accidents still do happen, but the vast majority of the time they are due to a recruit's error, not to negligence on the part of training personnel. Be sure you pay close attention to all safety briefings and that you follow all instructions to the letter.

If you get injured or get sick, you will be allowed to visit a doctor. He or she will determine how serious your injury or illness is. For less severe injuries or illnesses, the doctor may prescribe a day or two of light duty or bed rest. Your company commanders will be informed of this decision and will know how to take care of you. Follow any instructions given to you so that you can get back into training shape as quickly as possible. Returning to full training too soon could lead to further damage to your body, which could delay your training.

Recruits who are too injured or too sick to continue training with their platoon will be given time to heal, but that time does not count towards training. If you miss too many days, you will probably be reverted back to join another company. Remember that this is for your safety and so that you have the opportunity to learn what you need to learn. Joining a new company midway through training is hard, but learning how to adapt to a new situation and how to become part of a new team is part of military life.

Uniforms and Supplies

When you check in at Arrival you will get your initial issue of clothing, gear, toiletries, and supplies. The initial issue covers everything from underwear to razor blades to running shoes to a three-ring binder. You will also get a debit card which can be used at the Coast Guard Exchange to buy supplies and toiletries as you run out. During your time in basic training, you'll be issued even more gear and uniforms. Some of what you are issued, especially your uniform, is yours; you are paying for it and you'll need it for the future. Other gear, such as your practice rifle, is only yours during your time in basic training. It will be returned to supplies for the next recruit to use once you graduate.

Basic Training — Eight Weeks of Hard Work

Coast Guard basic training lasts eight weeks and can be broken down into six basic stages: arrival, company formation, learning the basics, practical training, preparation for your first unit, graduation. Arrival takes place when you first get to Cape May; see Chapter 19 for more information. Company formation and indoctrination weekend (also covered in Chapter 19) set the groundwork for you to learn the basics of being a member of the Coast Guard. After about two weeks of basics, you then move on to practical, hands-on training. As your practical training progresses, you then receive your orders to your first duty station and begin preparing to graduate and become a full-fledged member of the Coast Guard.

Eight weeks sounds like a lot of time — and it is — but there are ways to help yourself see the time passing. Set short, medium, and long-term goals. The short term is easiest: give each day your best effort. For a medium goal, focus on getting through the week, learning as much as you can. Your longest term goal is obviously to graduate successfully, but you should also focus on the end of the current stage. Each stage has a specific focus, which will help you see your learning progression during that stage. Learning the basics is just that, practical training focuses on learning how to do the work of a Guardian, and preparing for your first unit wraps up what you have learned and gives you a chance to practice behaving as a member of the armed forces. As you move through the stages, you will begin to see how what you are learning all fits together.

Learning the Basics

Indoctrination weekend begins the process of teaching you the basics of being a Guardian. You've already been in basic training for a week—being yelled at and ordered about since you got to Sexton Hall roughly six days ago—but now things will get even more intense. From here on out you must complete the assignments, pass the tests, and learn the information presented to you over the next few weeks or you will not graduate on time.

Learning the basics is focused on teaching you the basics of being a Guardian—how to march, how to wear a uniform, how the Coast Guard is organized, and how the Coast Guard expect you to behave. You will take classes in Coast Guard history, learning about the work the Coast Guard has done over the years and the people who have led and shaped the Coast Guard. You will participate in discussions of the Coast Guard Core Values: Honor, Respect, and Devotion to Duty. Each of these values is discussed in depth individually over the course of basic training, both by classroom teachers and by your company commanders. There will be classroom courses on military drill, military customs and courtesies, nautical terminology, military ranks, the Coast Guard's mission, and more. By then end of week two, you will be expected to be able to immediately answer questions about addressing Coast Guard personnel, Coast Guard terminology, the General Orders of a Sentry, military time, the phonetic alphabet, saluting, standing at attention, and more. (To prepare for basic training by learning some of these things in advance, see Chapter 15: Preparing for Basic Training.)

During this time you won't just be sitting in a classroom. You will also be doing daily physical fitness, including running and strengthening exercises. Some of that physical fitness will take place outdoors, but weather on Cape May can be unpredictable. On days when the weather is not suited for outdoor exercise, you'll head to the gym to work out on machines, both weight-lifting machines and cardio ones.

At the end of week two, you'll take your initial fitness assessment.

Because of the weather in Cape May, some of your physical fitness workouts will be held indoors (Official U.S. Coast Guard photograph by Chief Warrant Officer Veronica Bandrowsky).

This test is designed to make sure that you are on track to pass the final physical fitness assessment required for graduation. In order to graduate you have to meet the following standards:

Event	Assessment Minimum — Men
Run	1.5 mile run in 12 min. 51 sec.
Push-ups (in 60 sec.)	29
Sit-ups (in 60 sec.)	38

Event	Assessment Minimum — Women
Run	1.5 mile run in 15 min. 26 sec.
Push-ups (in 60 sec.)	23
Sit-ups (in 60 sec.)	32

If, after you take your initial fitness assessment, your company commanders do not think that you are able to meet those standards, then you will be assigned to Physical Fitness Enhancement, which means you will have to wake up an hour earlier than your fellow recruits to do a special fitness session.

Also at the end of week two you will fill out your dream sheet. The dream sheet is your list of places where you would like to go for your first assignment. They are not guaranteed to you, but the Coast Guard will consider your requests. For more information on what happens after basic training, see Chapter 22: Graduation and Beyond.

Practical Training

After you master the basic Coast Guard knowledge, then you move from classroom training onto more hands-on training. During this stage you learn how to fight fires, how to fire a weapon, how to handle lines and other seamanship skills, and more. This doesn't mean that classroom lessons stop, however. You'll still have plenty of those, focusing on insignia, vessels, aircraft, pay and allowances, equipment, and more. In week four you will take your written mid-term exam. This exam covers all of the classroom knowledge you have learned up to this point.

Even though you do not have to qualify with a weapon in order to graduate from the Coast Guard, you will still receive weapons training. The first part of weapons training is getting used to carrying around a non-firing rifle. The rifle is used in drill and as part of your physical fitness. Since the rifle has had its barrel filled with lead, it adds a new component to your incentive training! In weeks three and four, you move on to learning how to handle a handgun. You'll have classroom lessons on handgun usage and safety and the fundamentals of marksmanship. You will also receive hands-on training in a simulator and with an instructor.

You will also continue to do physical fitness training. During this stage you will get a chance to fight with Pugil Sticks. Pugil Sticks look like oversized Q-Tips and they are designed to simulate combat with a bayonet, a blade that attaches to the front of a rifle, and to teach you

Instructors will make sure you know the basics of handgun usage (Official U.S. Coast Guard photograph by Lt. j.g. Michael Cole)

how to attack and defend. Recruits are paired off and try to use the sticks to knock each other out of the ring. It can look brutal, but it is a great way of working out aggression! Another fun way to get motivated and in shape at the same time is the Confidence Course. The Confidence Course is an oversized obstacle course designed to physically challenge recruits and also to show them that they can accomplish difficult goals through hard work.

You will have to pass a fitness assessment in order to graduate. You will be tested in week two to make sure you are on the right track to pass, but the actual assessment is given around week four or five. In order to graduate you have to meet the following standards:

Event	Assessment Minimum — Men
Run	1.5 mile run in 12 min. 51 sec.
Push-ups (in 60 sec.)	29
Sit-ups (in 60 sec.)	38

Event	Assessment Minimum — Women
Run	1.5 mile run in 15 min. 26 sec.
Push-ups (in 60 sec.)	23
Sit-ups (in 60 sec.)	32

If you do not pass the assessment when you take it the first time, you will receive another shot at it in week seven, but you have to pass it then or you will not graduate.

The Coast Guard is a force that operates in and around the water. Therefore all recruits must pass at least basic swim qualification. To do so you have to jump off of a six-foot platform into the water, swim 100 meters, and tread water for five minutes. You will get more than one chance to pass the swim test, but you have to pass it in order to graduate. The Coast Guard will teach you how to swim if you don't already know how, but it is to your advantage to learn if you have a fear of water

Even as basic training is wrapping up, you will still be learning important skills, such as firefighting (Official U.S. Coast Guard photograph by Petty Officer 2nd Class Christopher D. McLaughlin).

before enlisting in the Coast Guard. (See Chapter 15 for other tips on preparing for recruit training.)

At the end of week five you will receive your orders for your first assignment after basic training. Your company commander will tell you where you have been assigned. At that time you'll have a chance to call your new duty station to make travel plans and also to call your family for the first time to tell them how you have been doing and where you'll be headed after graduation.

Preparing for Your First Unit

As you move through basic training, you will see that your company commanders are beginning to treat you less like an annoyance who cannot obey orders and more like an adult. This is part of the way that the Coast Guard shapes basic training. In the beginning you are subject to high amounts of stress, but as you progress through the stages of basic training and you learn how to behave as a Guardian, you are given more freedom and more respect. Towards the end of basic training, usually around week six, you will even earn a day of on-base liberty (or time off), assuming you and your company are performing well.

The last couple of weeks of Coast Guard basic training are focused on transitioning you from being a recruit to being a Guardian. You will still have classroom lessons, covering not only practical training such as seamanship, but also information you will need to know to plan your career, such as information on ratings and military entitlements. You will have a drill evaluation and a final written exam which will cover all of the information you have learned over the course of basic training. If you did not qualify in swimming or physical fitness when you were tested on them previously, you will have to qualify now or be reverted to another company.

Assuming you pass your exams and that you and your company have been performing up to your company commander's standards, then you will be granted a pass for off-base liberty on the Saturday of week seven. This means that you will be able to leave the training center and travel around Cape May. During your time off-base, you are expected to act like a Guardian at all times. All recruits celebrate their temporary freedom differently. Some get a hotel room and spend the day lounging in bed watching television. Others go to the movies or out to eat. Some even buy disposable cellphones and spend their 12 hours on the phone! Whatever you choose to do, be sure to maintain proper behavior. Even at this late stage of training, messing up can mean being reverted and missing graduation with your company.

After your liberty day, you'll spend your last few days at Cape May finalizing your travel plans to your new unit and preparing for graduation. Soon graduation day will be here and you'll be a proud new member of the United States Coast Guard.

Graduation and Beyond

The last week of basic training is spent wrapping up the final details of your training, returning any gear you are not keeping after training, and getting ready to travel to your new assignment. On the Thursday before graduation your company and the other companies that are graduating that day will have a practice march and graduation ceremony. Afterward there will be a special lunch of pizza or sandwiches. This lunch will be more relaxed than any of your other meals at Cape May. You'll be allowed to talk and you'll have a whole 30 minutes to eat and socialize, rather than your usual 15 minutes to eat in silence. Meanwhile your family and friends who are attending Graduation the next day can go to an inexpensive buffet dinner and get the chance to meet the family and friends of your fellow graduates.

Graduation

Graduation takes place outdoors in good weather and indoors in poor weather. As of Fall 2011, Cape May Training Center is renovating its indoor Graduation facility, so indoor graduations have been moved to the Performing Arts Center in town. Your company commander will keep you notified of where Graduation will be held for your company. Graduation takes place on Friday of your last training week, except for when that Friday is a holiday; then Graduation will be scheduled on an earlier day. It starts at 11 A.M. and lasts about forty-five minutes. Before Graduation starts there is a Parents' Briefing at 10 A.M. which tells your guests all about basic training.

Your Graduation ceremony is a proud moment. Recruits who have

A mom happily hugs her son, a newly graduated member of the Coast Guard (Official U.S. Coast Guard photograph by CWO Donnie Brzuska).

distinguished themselves in various ways will be recognized, as will any visiting dignitaries. If you have a friend or family member who is active duty military or another type of service member such as a police officer, then he or she is welcome to present you with your graduation certificate, as long as he or she wears his or her uniform to your ceremony.

There are a few tips to help make the day more enjoyable:

- *Don't make travel plans too early.* Your family should not make arrangements until you alert them to do so (usually during the fifth week of training, about when you find out your permanent duty assignment). There are a lot of things that can delay your training and they won't want to have to try to change plane tickets or hotel reservations if your graduation day changes. You will have arranged your own final travel details during your preparation for your first unit, so you will have a

201

way to get home after Graduation and a way to get to your new duty station.

- *Arrive early.* Remind your family that they will have to check in on base in order to be allowed to visit, so they need to allow time for that.
- *Dress for the weather.* Cape May can be cold for much of the year and very windy, even in summer months. Remind your family to bring sunscreen, sunglasses, hats, and other protection, as well as water bottles so they do not get dehydrated, for summer graduations, and warm clothes for winter ones. If it is raining, snowing, or very cold, Graduation will be moved indoors.
- *Dress appropriately.* Families can either dress up for the ceremony, just as they would for a high school or college graduation, or they may choose to wear shirts with your company information on it. Either is appropriate and acceptable.
- *Bring something to occupy small children.* Graduation is not long, but the ceremony can be too dry for small children. Bring books or small, quiet toys to keep them occupied.
- *Obey all traffic laws.* Speed limits on base are often very slow, usually 15–25 miles per hour. The Coast Guard takes these speed limits very seriously and your family will be pulled over if they violate them.
- *Include fellow Guardians whose families cannot come.* There will probably be at least one member of your company whose family cannot make it to graduation. Include him or her as a part of your family — after all, you are both Guardians now.

If your family cannot come to graduation because of financial reasons, there are often groups who might be able to help. Check with your house of worship or local Coast Guard reserve unit to see if they might have a program to assist families in attending graduation.

Once the Graduation ceremony is over, you will have to return to your squad bay to pick up your gear. Your family and friends are welcome to come with you and take a tour of the base. Then you are officially on leave (vacation) for five days, starting the Saturday after Graduation.

After Graduation

And now you are a Guardian. Congratulations! But your journey has just begun. After enjoying your five days of leave, you will leave for your new permanent duty assignment, the one you were assigned to in week five. You'll be an undesignated seaman, fireman, or airman and, as such, you will be charged with doing whatever your commanding officers decide they need you to do. The advantage of this is that you will be able to sample all of the different types of jobs available in the Coast Guard before you decide which one might be right for you. After two or three years at your first duty station, you can apply to one of the Coast Guard's sixteen "A" Schools for formal training in a specific job or you can try to "strike" for a job (called a "rating"). Striking is a challenging combination of on-the-job training and self-study and is available for five of the Coast Guard's ratings. No matter which you chose, by the time you enter further training, you'll already be a proud Guardian.

Glossary of Military Terms

Active Duty— those military personnel who serve full time

AFQT: The Armed Forces Qualifying Test— a part of the ASVAB; made up of four tests that measure your knowledge of math and language skills; the AFQT used to determine your eligibility for military enlistment

Air Force— the branch of the military responsible for air warfare

Allowances— moneys which help military personnel pay for housing, food, uniforms, etc.

Army— the branch of the military responsible for land warfare

ASVAB: the Armed Services Vocational Aptitude Battery— a series of tests taken to determine your skills and knowledge; used for job placement in the military

Barracks— dormitory style housing on military bases

Basic Training or Recruit Training (also called Boot Camp)— the initial training for new enlisted military personnel; lasts between seven and thirteen weeks depending upon the branch of the service

CAST: Computer Adaptive Screening Test or *EST: Enlistment Screening Test*— a mini–ASVAB test taken in a recruiter's office which shows what a potential enlistee's AFQT score will probably be; used to help potential enlistees know if their scores will qualify them for enlistment

CAT: Computer Adaptive Test— name of the ASVAB test when taken on computer

Chaplain— the military term for a religious leader, preacher, minister, rabbi, imam, etc.

Civilians— those persons not serving in the military

Coast Guard—the branch of the military responsible for law enforcement on the waters (lakes, rivers, etc.) in and around the United States

Commissary—a grocery store on a military base

Conscientious Objector—someone who refuses to fight or participate in any war because of religious, personal, moral, or ethical beliefs

DEP: Delayed Entry Program—the period of time between finalizing the enlistment process and leaving for basic training; length varies from a few weeks to 365 days

Dependents—any people that a military person has to take care of: a spouse, any children or stepchildren (living in the home) who are under 18 and unmarried, and any other family members who rely on a military member for more than half of their support

DoD: Department of Defense—the government agency that oversees four branches of the military—Air Force, Army, Navy, Marines; the Coast Guard is under the Department of Homeland Security

Don't Ask, Don't Tell—a policy put in place in 1993 which allowed homosexuals to serve in the military, but only if they did not tell anyone their sexual orientation or participate in homosexual activities (i.e., sex or gay marriage); overturned in December 2010; fully repealed in September 2011

Enlisted—those military personnel who are responsible for the daily operations of the military under the command of officers; ranks range from E-1 to E-9

Enlistment Process—the steps taken to join the military as an enlisted person

Exchange—a department or general goods store on a military base

Incentive Pay—special pay which some military personnel earn because of the job they do or the risks to which they are exposed

IRR: Individual Ready Reserve—former military personnel who do not drill or receive pay, but who can still be called up to active duty; the last years of an enlistment are spent in the IRR

Marine Corps—the branch of the military responsible for amphibious (sea-to-land) warfare

MEPS: Military Entrance Processing Station— a Department of Defense facility that is in charge of physical and mental exams of potential enlistees, as well as administering the Oath of Enlistment and shipping new recruits off to basic training

MET: Mobile Examining Team— a facility that exists solely to administer the ASVAB test to potential enlistees

MOS: Military Occupational Specialty— the job field you will be assigned and trained in

MRE: Meal-Ready-to-Eat— portable, long-lasting, prepackaged meal eaten during field maneuvers and combat

National Guard— the reserve military programs that are managed by individual states, rather than by the Federal Government; there are two: Army National Guard and Air National Guard (Air Force)

Navy— the branch of the military responsible for warfare on the sea

NCOs: Non-commissioned officers— the upper enlisted ranks; NCOs act as leaders and managers; generally the ranks of E-4 to E-9, with E-4 to E-6 called junior NCOs and E-7 to E-9 called senior NCOs

Oath of Enlistment— the official swearing-in pledge that all new recruits take just before leaving for basic training

Officers— the command personnel of the military branches; ranks range from O-1 to O-9

PAP: Paper and Pencil— name of the ASVAB test taken on paper

Pay grade— the level of pay a particular military member is eligible for each month

Post–9/11 GI Bill— the most commonly used education programs for all branches of the military; it provides money for tuition and other expenses

Rank— the position you hold within the military; can be enlisted, warrant officer, or officer

Recruit Company Commander—the Coast Guard term for the person in charge of recruits during recruit training

Recruiter— the military man or woman who is responsible for giving out information about joining the military, finding candidates for enlistment, checking their qualifications, guiding them through the enlistment process, and offering tips on how to prepare for recruit training

Reserves—those military personnel who serve part-time, training one weekend a month and two weeks a year; they can be called up to active duty when needed

Stop Loss—a program which allows the military, during times of conflict, to prevent personnel from leaving the military on their normal separation date for up to one year; used during times of war to keep needed personnel on active duty

Technical Subtests—a part of the ASVAB; made up of five tests that measure your knowledge of and aptitude (natural talent) for technical skills; the technical subtests are used to determine which jobs you are eligible for

Tricare—the military's health care plan

UCMJ: Uniform Code of Military Justice—the official military laws of the United States, parts of which cover the criminal prosecution of military personnel

USO: United Services Organizations, Inc.—a private, nonprofit group that support military personnel by providing morale, welfare, and recreational services

Waiver—official approval that allows someone to enlist in the military despite not meeting a particular qualification or qualifications

Warrant Officers—a specialty rank that falls in-between enlisted personnel and officers; the Air Force is the only branch that does not have Warrant Officers

For More Information

Further Information about the Coast Guard and the United States Military

BOOKS

Bonner, Kit, and Carolyn. *Always Ready: Today's U.S. Coast Guard*. The Power Series. St. Paul, MN: MBI, 2004.

Coast Guard Publication 1— U.S. Coast Guard: America's Maritime Guardian. 2009. Download at *http://www.uscg.mil/TOP/ABOUT/PUB1.ASP.*

A Day in the Life of the United States Armed Forces. New York: Epicom Media, 2003.

Dolan, Edward F. *Careers in the U.S. Coast Guard*. Military Service. New York: Marshall Cavendish/Benchmark, 2010.

The Guardian Handbook. 2010. Download at *http://www.uscg.mil/hq/capemay/docs/GuardianHandbookfinal%20.pdf.*

Helvarg, David. *Rescue Warriors: The U.S. Coast Guard, America's Forgotten Heroes*. New York: Thomas Dunne, 2009.

Kroll, C. Douglas. *A Coast Guardsman's History of the U.S. Coast Guard*. Annapolis, MD: Naval Institute Press, 2010.

Schading, Barbara. *A Civilian's Guide to the U.S. Military: A Comprehensive Reference to the Customs, Language, and Structure of the Armed Forces*. Cincinnati, OH: Writer's Digest, 2007.

VIDEOS

Inside Today's Military: *http://www.todaysmilitary.com/inside.*

United States Coast Guard's Visual Information Gallery: *http://cgvi.uscg.mil/media/main.php.*

WEBSITES

About.com's U.S. Military site: *http://usmilitary.about.com.*

Department of Homeland Security's Official Site: *http://www.dhs.gov.*

Military.com: *http://www.military.com*. [NOTE: To access some information on Military.com, you will have to register and your information will be shared with recruiters.]

Military Woman: *http://www.militarywoman.org*.

Today's Military: *http://www.todaysmilitary.com*.

United States Coast Guard's Official Site: *http://www.uscg.mil*.

Military Career Planning

BOOKS

Careers in Focus: Armed Forces. New York: Ferguson, 2008.

Goldberg, Jan. *Careers for Patriotic Types and Others Who Want to Serve Their Country*. Careers for You. 2nd edition. New York: McGraw-Hill, 2006.

Henderson, C.J., and Jack Dolphin. *Career Opportunities in the Armed Forces*. 2nd edition. Revised by Pamela Fehl. New York: Ferguson, 2007.

150 Best Jobs Through Military Training. Indianapolis, IN: JIST, 2008.

Sterngass, Jon. *Armed Forces*. Great Careers with a High School Diploma. New York: Ferguson, 2008.

WEBSITES

ASVAB Career Exploration Program: *http://www.asvabprogram.com*.

Military Career Information: *http://usmilitary.about.com/od/theorderlyroom/u/career_info.htm*.

Military Careers: *http://www.todaysmilitary.com/careers*.

My Future: *http://www.myfuture.com*. [This is a Department of Defense website that brings together information about careers, colleges, and military service provided by the Departments of Commerce, Defense, Education and Labor.]

Military Benefits

BOOK

Michel, Christopher P., and Terry Howell. *The Military Advantage: The Military.com Guide to Military and Veterans Benefits*. 2010 edition. Annapolis, MD: Naval Institute Press, 2010.

WEBSITES

Defense Finance and Accounting Service — Military Pay: *http://www.dfas.mil/militarypay.html*.

Department of Veterans Affairs' GI Bill Site: *http://www.gibill.va.gov.*

Department of Veterans Affairs' Jack-of-All-Trades page: *http://www.gibill.va. gov/bill-of-all-trades/index.html.* [Gives information on non-college programs that are supported by the GI Bill.]

Department of Veterans Affairs' WEAMS Institution Search: *http://inquiry. vba.va.gov/weamspub/buildSearchInstitutionCriteria.do.* [Allows you to search for continuing education programs which will be covered by the GI Bill.]

Military Benefits: *http://www.military.com/Benefits* and *http://www.myfuture. com/military/articles-advice/military-benefits.*

Military Pay and Benefits: *http://usmilitary.about.com/od/militarypay/u/pay_ and_benefits.htm.*

So Much More Than Just a Paycheck: *http://www.todaysmilitary.com/benefits.*

Understanding the Post–9/11 GI Bill: *http://images.military.com/media/education/pdf/post911_gibill.pdf.*

United States Coast Guard — Pay Rates and Benefits: *http://www.uscg.mil/ ppc/rates.asp.*

Enlistment Information

BOOK

Ostrow, Scott. *Guide to Joining the Military.* 2nd edition. Lawrenceville, NJ: ARCO, 2003.

VIDEO

A Day at the MEPS: *http://www.mepcom.army.mil/video.html.*

WEBSITES

U.S. Coast Guard's Official Recruiting Site: *http://www.gocoastguard.com.*

10 Steps to Joining the Military: *http://www.military.com/Recruiting.*

Joining the Military: *http://usmilitary.about.com/od/joiningthemilitary/u/ joining_up.htm.*

Coast Guard Recruiting

Use this contact information to report inappropriate behavior on the part of a recruiter.

Telephone: (887) 669–8724

Mail: 2300 Wilson Blvd. Suite 500, Arlington, VA 20598–7500

ASVAB: Information and Study Guides

Books

Ostrow, Scott A. *Master the ASVAB.* 21st ed. Lawrenceville, NJ: Thomson/
Arco, 2008. [Includes information on military careers.]
Powers, Rod. *ASVAB AFQT for Dummies.* Hoboken, NJ: Wiley, 2010.
Powers, Rod, and Jennifer Lawler. *ASVAB for Dummies.* 2nd ed. Hoboken,
NJ: Wiley, 2007. [Includes information on which subtests correspond to
which military job.]
Stradley, Laura, and Robin Kavanagh. *The Complete Idiot's Guide to the
ASVAB: Time-Tested Techniques for Acing the ASVAB!* New York: Alpha,
2010.

Websites

ASVAB Career Exploration Program: *http://www.asvabprogram.com.*
ASVAB's Official Site: *http://www.official-asvab.com.*
March2Success: *https://www.march2success.com.* [A test-prep site developed
by the U.S. Army.]

Life During Coast Guard Recruit Training

Books

Powers, Rod. *Basic Training for Dummies.* Hoboken, NJ: Wiley, 2011.
Recruit Training Pocket Guide. 2010. Download at *http://www.uscg.mil/hq/
capemay/docs/RecruitTrainingPocketGuide.pdf.* [This has much of the information that you'll be expected to learn while at Coast Guard basic training.]
The Helmsman. Download at *http://www.uscg.mil/hq/capemay/docs/pdf%20
docs/Helmsmannew.pdf.*
Helvarg, David. *Rescue Warriors: The U.S. Coast Guard, America's Forgotten
Heroes.* New York: Thomas Dunne, 2009. [See Chapter 2 in *Rescue Warriors* for information on Coast Guard Basic Training.]

Videos

Basic Training Interview Series: *http://www.gocoastguard.com/serving-in-the-
u.s.-coast-guard/basic-training/basic-training-interview-series.*
"It's Just Eight Weeks," Coast Guard Basic Training: *http://www.youtube.
com/watch?v=6i8PX3fyF0k.*

Recruit Travel Video: *http://www.mepcom.army.mil/travel-video.html.* [Tells new recruits the procedures that should be followed while traveling to basic training.]

WEBSITES

USCG Training Center, Cape May, NJ — Official Site: *http://www.uscgboot-camp.com.*

Coast Guard Basic Training: *http://www.gocoastguard.com/serving-in-the-u.s.-coast-guard/basic-training.*

"Surviving Military Boot Camp: Part VI — Coast Guard Basic Training" at About.com's U.S. Military site: *http://usmilitary.about.com/od/cgjoin/l/aacg-basic1.htm.*

For Younger Readers

BOOKS

Benson, Michael. *The U.S. Coast Guard.* U.S. Armed Forces. Minneapolis, MN: Lerner, 2005.

Demarest, Chris L. *Alpha Bravo Charlie: The Military Alphabet.* New York: Margaret K. McElderry Books, 2005.

Hamilton, John. *The Coast Guard.* Defending the Nation. Edina, MN: Abdo, 2007.

WEBSITE

Coast Guard Coloring Books: *http://www.uscg.mil/top/downloads/coloring .asp.*

Resources

Allen, Admiral Thad, USCG. "Identity of the Guardian." *Leadership Journal Archives*. Department of Homeland Security, 2008. http://www.dhs.gov/journal/leadership/2008/08/identity-of-guardian.html.

Allison, Aimee, and David Solnit. *Army of None: Strategies to Counter Military Recruitment, End War, and Build a Better World*. New York: Seven Stories, 2007.

American Women and the United States Armed Forces: A Guide to the Records of Military Agencies in the National Archives Relating to American Women. Compiled by Charlotte Palmer Seeley. Revised by Virginia C. Purdy and Robert Gruber. Washington, DC: National Archives and Records Administration, 1992.

Ashabranner, Brent. *A Date with Destiny: The Women in Military Service for America Memorial*. Photographs by Jennifer Ashabranner. Great American Memorials series. Brookfield, CT: Twenty-first Century Books, 2000.

Baker, Anni. *Life in the U.S. Armed Forces: (Not) Just Another Job*. Westport, CT: Praeger Security International, 2008.

Benson, Michael. *The U.S. Coast Guard*. U.S. Armed Forces. Minneapolis, MN: Lerner, 2005.

Bonner, Kit, and Carolyn. *Always Ready: Today's U.S. Coast Guard*. The Power Series. St. Paul, MN: MBI, 2004.

Bradford, James C., ed. *International Encyclopedia of Military History*. New York: Routledge, 2006.

Buckley, Gail. *American Patriots: The Story of Blacks in the Military from the Revolution to Desert Storm*. Adapted by Tonya Bolden. New York: Crown, 2003.

Burns, Robert. "Ask and Tell: 18-year Ban of Gays in Military is Lifted." *Charlotte Observer*, September 21, 2011, sec. A.

_____. "Military Is 'Adequately Prepared' to End Ban on Gays, Says Pentagon." *Charlotte Observer*, September 20, 2011, sec. A.

Careers in Focus: Armed Forces. New York: Ferguson, 2008.

Chambers, John Whiteclay II, ed. *The Oxford Companion to American Military History.* New York: Oxford University Press, 1999.

Collins, Robert F. *Basic Training: What to Expect and How to Prepare.* Military Opportunity. New York: Rosen, 1988.

Defense Finance and Accounting Service. "Military Pay Tables — 1949 to 2011." http://www.dfas.mil/militarymembers/payentitlements/military-paytables.html.

Department of Defense. *Personnel & Procurement Reports and Data Files.* DoD Personnel & Procurement Statistics. http://siadapp.dmdc.osd.mil.

Department of Homeland Security. *Organizational Chart.* 2010. http://www.dhs.gov/xabout/structure/editorial_0644.shtm.

Dillon, C. Hall. "The Military Offers Valuable Training for Civilian Careers." In *Choosing a Career*, edited by Linda Aksomitis. Issues That Concern You. Detroit: Gale, 2008.

Dolan, Edward F. *Careers in the U.S. Coast Guard.* Military Service. New York: Marshall Cavendish/Benchmark, 2010.

Doubler, Michael D. *The National Guard and Reserve: A Reference Handbook.* Contemporary Military, Strategic, and Security Issues. Westport, CT: Praeger Security International, 2008.

Dribben, Melissa. "Sexual Assault a Silent Battle for Servicewomen." *Charlotte Observer*, September 18, 2011, sec. A.

Gavin, Lettie. *American Women in World War I: They Also Served.* Niwot: University Press of Colorado, 1997.

Gibbs, Nancy. "Sexual Assaults on Female Soldiers: Don't Ask, Don't Tell." *Time,* March 8, 2010. http://www.time.com/time/magazine/article/0,91 71,1968110,00.html.

Goldberg, Jan. *Careers for Patriotic Types and Others Who Want to Serve Their Country.* Careers for You. 2nd ed. New York: McGraw-Hill, 2006.

Goldstein, Joshua S. *War and Gender: How Gender Shapes the War System and Vice Versa.* Cambridge: Cambridge University Press, 2001.

Hamilton, John. *The Coast Guard.* Defending the Nation. Edina, MN: Abdo, 2007.

Harris, Bill. *The Complete Idiot's Guide to Careers in the Military.* Indianapolis, IN: Alpha, 2002.

Helvarg, David. *Rescue Warriors: The U.S. Coast Guard, America's Forgotten Heroes.* New York: Thomas Dunne Books, 2009.

Henderson, C.J., and Jack Dolphin. *Career Opportunities in the Armed Forces.* 2nd ed. Revised by Pamela Fehl. New York: Ferguson, 2007.

Herbert, Don. *63 Days and a Wake-Up: Your Survival Guide to United States Army Basic Combat Training.* New York: iUniverse, 2007.

Kilpatrick, Kelly. "Things to Consider Before Joining the US Military." *US Military.* About.com. http://usmilitary.about.com/od/joiningthemilitary/a/consider.htm.

Leff, Lisa. "Active-Duty Gays: Coming Out Has Been Nonevent." *Army Times,* October 16, 2011. http://www.armytimes.com/news/2011/10/ap-military-dont-ask-dont-tell-gays-coming-out-nonevent-101611.

Michel, Christopher P., and Terry Howell. *The Military Advantage: The Military.com Guide to Military and Veterans Benefits.* 2010 ed. Annapolis, MD: Naval Institute Press, 2010.

Military.com. "Learn to Use Your GI Bill Benefits." *Education.* http://www.military.com/education/content/gi-bill/learn-to-use-your-gi-bill.html.

_____. "Military Benefits." *Benefits.* http://www.military.com/Benefits.

MilitarySpot.com. "Basic Training in the Coast Guard." http://www.militaryspot.com/coast-guard/basic-training-in-the-coast-guard.

Nathan, Amy. *Count on Us: American Women in the Military.* Washington, DC: National Geographic Society, 2004.

Ordoñez, Franco. "Military Gets Ready for a New Era." *Charlotte Observer,* August 28, 2011, sec. A.

Ostrom, Thomas P. *The United States Coast Guard: 1790 to the Present, a History.* Revised Edition. Oakland, OR: Red Anvil, 2006.

Ostrow, Scott A. *Guide to Joining the Military.* 2nd ed. Lawrenceville, NJ: Thomson/Arco, 2004.

_____. *Master the ASVAB.* 21st ed. Lawrenceville, NJ: Thomson/Arco, 2008.

Paradis, Adrian A. *Opportunities in Military Careers.* Rev. ed. New York: McGraw-Hill, 2006.

Parker, Ashley. "Lawsuit Says Military Is Rife with Sexual Abuse." *The New York Times,* February 15, 2011. http://www.nytimes.com/2011/02/16/us/16military.html.

Philpott, Tom. "Gay Benefits Rules Drafted." *Headlines.* Military.com, December 2, 2010. http://www.military.com/features/0,15240,223455,00.html.

Porterfield, Jason. *Frequently Asked Questions About College and Career Training.* Teen Life. New York: Rosen, 2009.

Powers, Rod. *Basic Training for Dummies.* Hoboken, NJ: Wiley, 2011.

_____. *US Military.* About.com. http://usmilitary.about.com.

_____, and Jennifer Lawler. *ASVAB for Dummies.* 2nd ed. Hoboken, NJ: Wiley, 2007.

Rosen, James. "First Lady to Visit Army Base in S.C." *Charlotte Observer*, January 24, 2011, sec. A.

Schading, Barbara. *A Civilian's Guide to the U.S. Military: A Comprehensive Reference to the Customs, Language, and Structure of the Armed Forces.* Cincinnati, OH: Writer's Digest, 2007.

Stalsburg, Brittany L. "After Repeal: LGBT Service Members and Veterans: The Facts." *Publications.* Service Women's Action Network, 2011. http://servicewomen.org/wp-content/uploads/2011/10/LGBT-Fact-Sheet-091411.pdf.

_____. "Rape, Sexual Assault and Sexual Harassment in the Military: The Quick Facts." *Publications.* Service Women's Action Network, 2011. http://servicewomen.org/wp-content/uploads/2011/09/R-SASH-Quick-Facts-081811.pdf.

Stewart, Gail B. *Fighting for Freedom: Blacks in the American Military.* Lucent Library of Black History. Detroit, MI: Thompson Gale, 2006.

Stradley, Laura, and Robin Kavanagh. *The Complete Idiot's Guide to the ASVAB: Time-Tested Techniques for Acing the ASVAB!* New York: Alpha, 2010.

Tate, Curtis. "Pentagon Lets Chaplains Perform Gay Weddings." The *Charlotte Observer,* October 1, 2011, sec. A.

Thompson, Peter. *The Real Insider's Guide to Military Basic Training: A Recruit's Guide of Important Secrets and Hints to Successfully Complete Boot Camp.* Rev. ed. Universal Publishers/uPUBLISH.com, 2002.

Understanding the Post–9/11 GI Bill. Military Advantage, 2009. http://images.military.com/media/education/pdf/post-911-gi-bill.pdf.

United States Army. "Symbols & Insignias." *Official Site.* http://www.army.mil/symbols.

United States Census Bureau. *Statistical Abstract.* http://www.census.gov/compendia/statab.

United States Coast Guard. *Official Site.* http://www.uscg.mil.

_____. *Recruiting Site.* http://www.gocoastguard.com.

United States Department of Veterans Affairs. *GI Bill Web Site.* http://www.gibill.va.gov/

United States Federal Government. "U.S. Code TITLE 6 > CHAPTER 1 > SUBCHAPTER VIII > Part H > § 468. Preserving Coast Guard Mission Performance." *Legal Information Institute.* Cornell University Law School. http://www.law.cornell.edu/uscode/6/468.html.

_____. "U.S. Code TITLE 10 > Subtitle C > PART I > CHAPTER 31 > § 502. Enlistment Oath: Who May Administer." *Legal Information Insti-*

tute. Cornell University Law School. http://www.law.cornell.edu/uscode/html/uscode10/usc_sec_10_00000502----000-.html.

United States Military Entrance Processing Command. *Enlistment Processing*. http://www.mepcom.army.mil/enlistment.html

_____. *USMEPCOM Videos*. http://www.mepcom.army.mil/MEPCOM_videos.html.

Vaughn, Kirby Lee. *The Enlistment Planning Guide: How to Make the Most of Your Military Service*. Santa Barbara, CA: Essayons, 1995.

Volkin, Sergeant Michael. *The Ultimate Basic Training Guidebook: Tips, Tricks, and Tactics for Surviving Boot Camp*. 4th ed. New York: Savas Beatie, 2009.

Watson, Cynthia A. *U.S. Military Service: A Reference Handbook*. Contemporary World Issues. Santa Barbara, CA: ABC-CLIO, 2007.

Watson, Julie. "For Gay Troops, Changes Precede End of DADT." *Marine Corps Times*, September 18, 2011. http://www.marinecorpstimes.com/news/2011/09/ap-for-gay-troops-changes-precede-end-of-dadt-091811.

Weill-Greenberg, Elizabeth, ed. *10 Excellent Reasons Not to Join the Military*. New York: The New Press, 2006.

Women in Military Service for America Memorial Foundation, Inc. "Statistics on Women in the Military." *For the Press*. http://www.womensmemorial.org/PDFs/StatsonWIM.pdf.

Youssef, Nancy A. "Military Outlines New Policy on Gays." The *Charlotte Observer*, January 29, 2011, sec. A.

Index

Numbers in **bold italics** indicate pages with photographs.

SAVL ³⁄₁₃